CRICUT PROJECT IDEAS

VOL. 1

HUNDREDS OF FABULOUS IDEAS FOR YOUR PROJECTS
CATEGORIZED BY MATERIAL TYPE

Made with love

by

Sienna

Tally

TABLE OF CONTENTS

INTRODUCTION   6

CHAPTER 1: WHAT DIFFERENT MATERIALS DO CRICUT MACHINES CUT?   8

CHAPTER 2: PAPER AND CARDSTOCK PROJECTS   15

Wedding Invitations   19
Custom Notebooks   21
Paper Flowers   22
Fruity Tray   26
Craft paper pencil holder   28
Birth announcement card   29
DIY Bookmark Cat-page   30
3d Paper Flowers (Paper)   33
Luminaries   34
Table Decoration   35

CHAPTER 3: VINYL PROJECTS   38

Vinyl Clock?   38
April Fools Gag Glass Decal   38
Snowman Lantern   42
Personalized Coaster Tiles   45
Customized Doormat   46
Glitter Tumbler   48
Vinyl Chalkboard   50
Vinyl Herringbone Bracelet   52
Treasure Chest Jewelry Box   55
Motivational Water Bottle   56
Customized Makeup Bag   57
Perpetual Calendar   58

CHAPTER 4: IRON ON AND HEAT TRANSFER VINYL (HTV) CRAFTS — 60

Personalized Mugs (Iron-On Vinyl) — 60
Halloween Pumpkin Vinyl Design — 63
Father's Day Mug — 63
Ice Cream Cones Covers — 65
Custom Graphic T-shirt? — 68
Customized Sock — 70
Halloween T-Shirt — 73
Shirts (Vinyl Iron On) — 76

CHAPTER 5: INFUSIBLE INK — 81

Dad Joke Vinyl T-Shirt — 81
Quiver and Arrow — 82
St. Patrick's Day Shirt — 83
Coasters using Infusible Ink for Christmas — 85
Clear Personalized Labels — 86
Custom Coasters — 89

CHAPTER 6: BASSWOOD, CHIPBOARD, BALSA WOOD — 92

Wooden Hand-Lettered Sign- — 92
Wooden Gift Tags- — 94
Charming Driftwood Sign- — 95
Party Decor Medallions- — 96
Chalkboard Calendar- — 98
Family Birthday Wooden Board- — 99

CONCLUSION — 102

INTRODUCTION — 102

Introduction

In the past, choosing a design could cause epic proportional migraines, but it's a different story now. The famous Cricut computer is responsible for cutting paper, vinyl, and cloth based on a specific pattern or design. The print or template can be produced or modified using a Cricut Design Studio program.

When you purchase your Cricut machine, you will be excited to get started. Search the online Cricut library for ideas on creating cool projects that will make your environment more enjoyable and a project that you can use to give others joy in their life, such as cards and wooden signs.

The craftier you are, the more fun this new machine that you have purchased will provide you. If you are ready to get crafting, then I suggest you take this book and the other manual that came with your Cricut and begin learning all the tools and tips that I have included. This will help bring you one step closer to being a master crafter when using your Cricut.

You can create your paper, allow it to dried up completely, then media with your iron (no steam).

You can use your paper to produce simple type scrapbooks or cards and one of your kind embellishments. Items nobody else has or will understand how to copy regardless of how difficult they try. This can allow your designs to create original scrapbooks using a range of colors and textures that can't be duplicated.

The chipboard shouldn't be worn, or you will damage the blades. You need to keep monitor of the edge's sharpness so that you can continuously enjoy an alternative if required.

Heavier grade of cardstock could cause blades to flat faster. This means you will have the chance to purchase thinner, more affordable paper or cardstock.

This book levels up your game up in the crafting business. The expert qualities that you shall learn from this book will take you on a journey of setting up your own business by making and selling wonderful Cricut designs. Now it is up to you to decide whether you want to step up your level to become a successful crafter of all time or you just want to stick to the basics. Expert level is the real thing in the crafting game. A lengthy illustrative five expert level projects are enough to equip you with every sort of powerful skill to enable you in the masters of Cricut designs. In this detailed guide, you'll discover the top project ideas to skyrocket with your Cricut Projects in 2021.

Chapter 1
What different materials do Cricut machines cut

Your Cricut Machine capabilities are influenced by the blades you are using (or can use with it). Depending on the edges you are using, you can cut more or fewer materials. Using the Cricut Explore Family machines, you can cut plenty of materials, most of them with the Premium Fine-Point Blade. Of course, when cutting the materials, you need to modify the cut pressure. If you have issues cutting that specific material and increasing the pressure doesn't solve the problems, you may need to adjust the blade depth.

Therefore, with a Cricut Machine from the Explore Series, you can cut the following materials:

- Paper (more or less thick)
- Vinyl
- Iron on
- Light cardstock
- Cardstock
- Fabric
- Posterboard
- distressed craft foam
- Plus craft foam
- Craft foam
- adhesive-backed cork

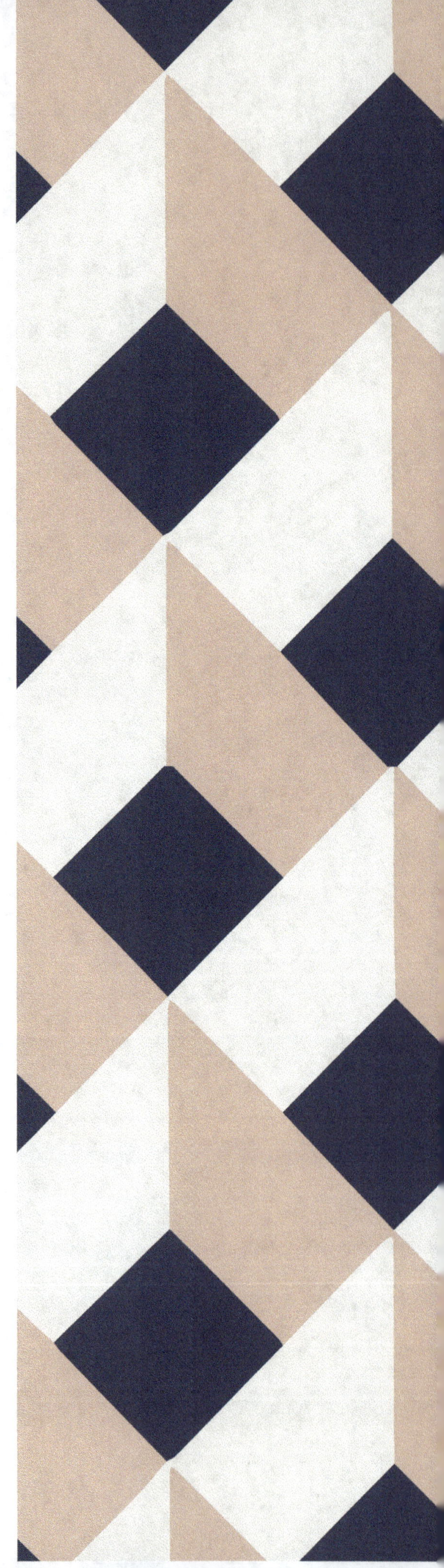

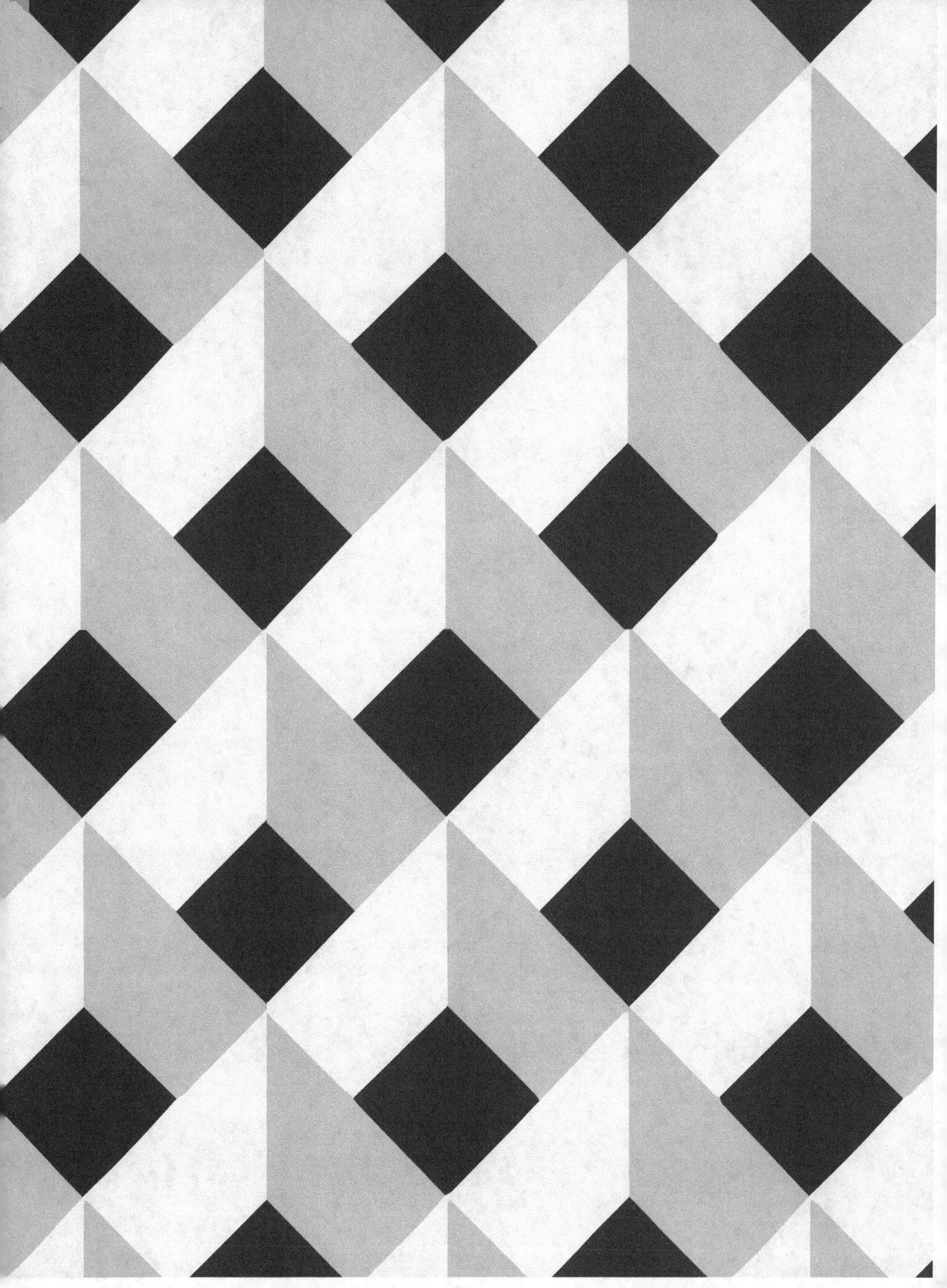

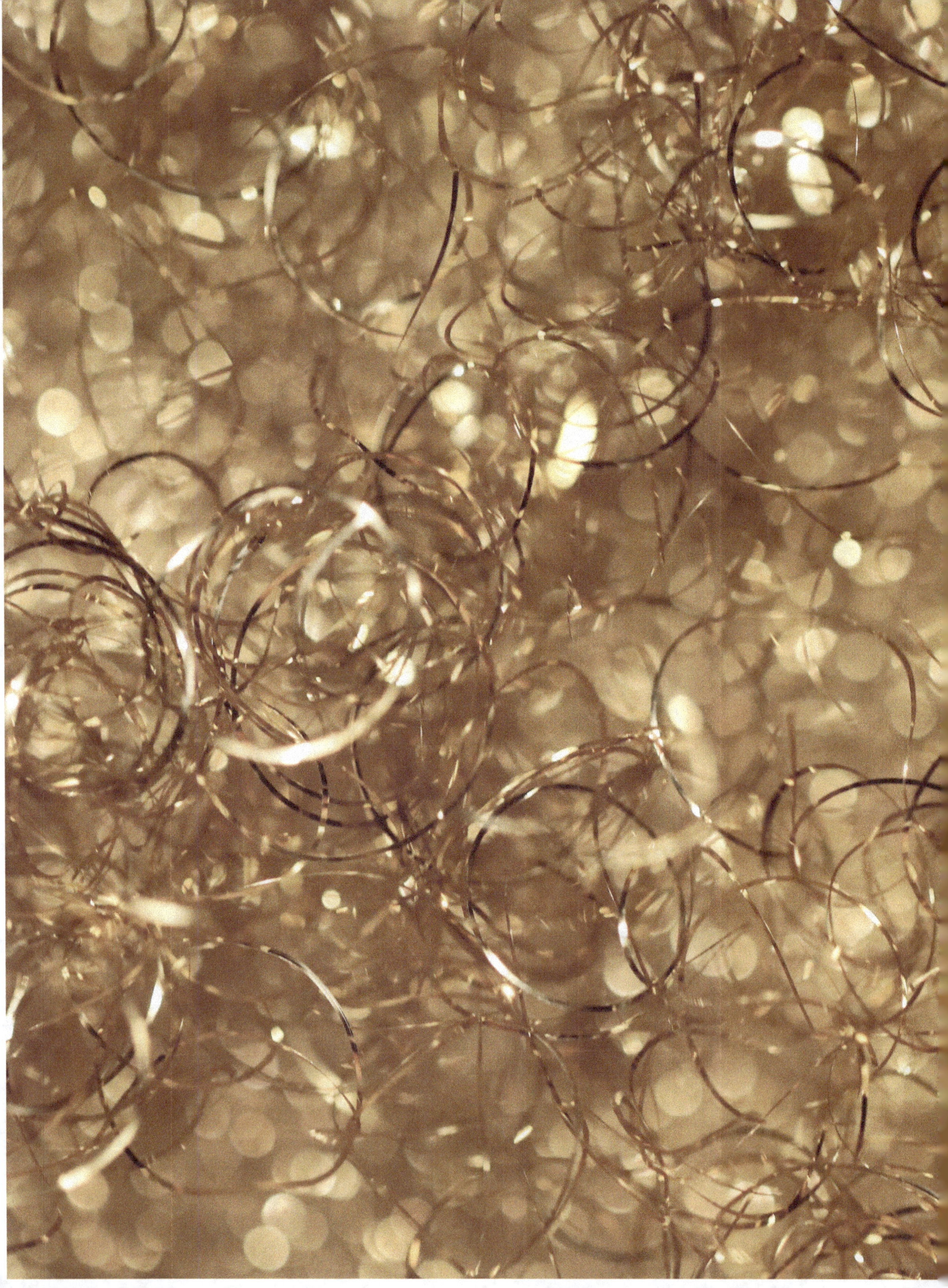

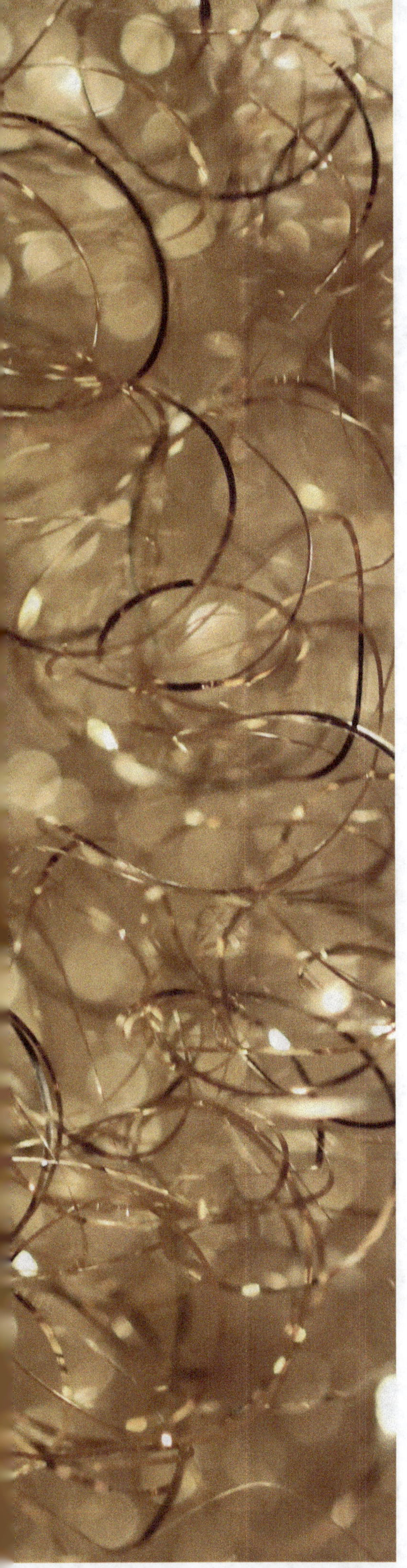

- Notebook paper
- wrapping paper
- Aluminum foil
- washi sheet
- iron-on holographic sparkle
- felt
- Epoxy Glitter paper
- Heavy watercolor paper (140 lb)
- Aluminum (0.14 mm)
- Glitter cardstock
- Wool fabric felt
- stencil film (0.4 mm)
- Garment leather (2-3 oz)
- Acetate
- Adhesive foil
- Matte adhesive foil
- Aluminum foil
- Balsa wood – 1/16"
- Bengaline
- Permanent adhesive birch
- Boucle
- Broadcloth
- Burlap
- Burn-out velvet
- Calico
- Cambric
- Canvas
- Carbon fiber
- Cardstock
  (for more intricate cuts)
- Adhesive-backed cardstock
- Cashmere
- Cereal box
- Chalkboard vinyl
- Challis

- Chambray
- Chantilly lace
- Charmeuse Satin
- Chiffon
- Chintz
- Clear Printable Sticker Paper
- Colored duct tape
- Copy paper – 20 lb
- Corduroy
- Corrugated cardboard
- Cotton
- Bonded cotton
- Craft foam
- Crepe Charmeuse
- Crepe de Chine
- Crepe Paper
- Crepe-back satin
- Cutting mat protector
- Damask
- Delicate fabrics (like Tulle)
- Deluxe paper
- Denim
- Bonded denim
- Dotted Swiss
- Double Cloth
- Double Knit
- Dry Erase Vinyl
- Flex Foam
- Gabardine
- Gauze
- Gel Sheet
- Genuine Leather
- Georgette
- Glitter Cardstock
- Glitter Craft Foam

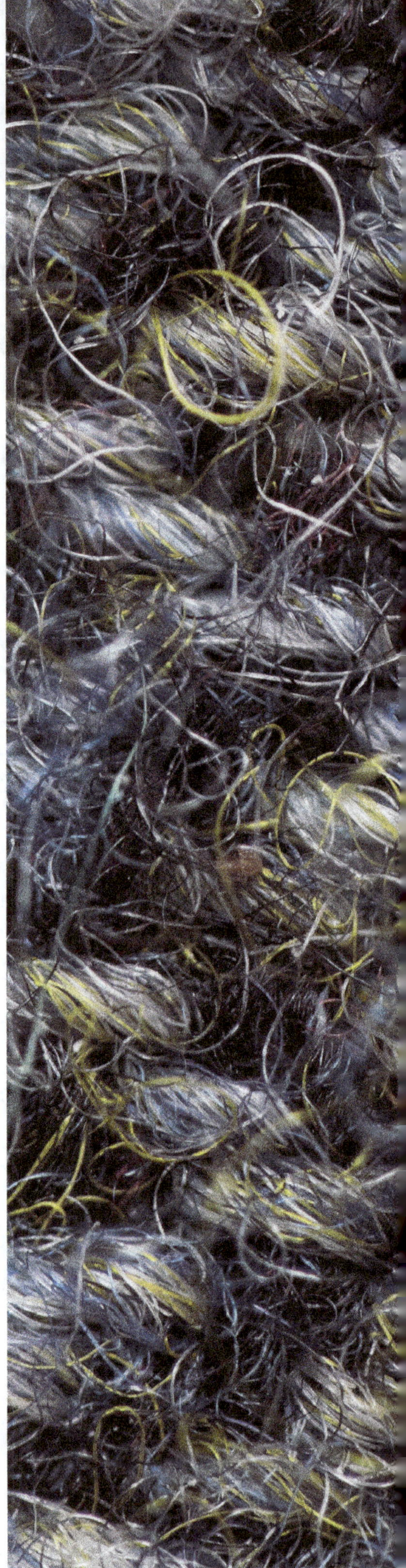

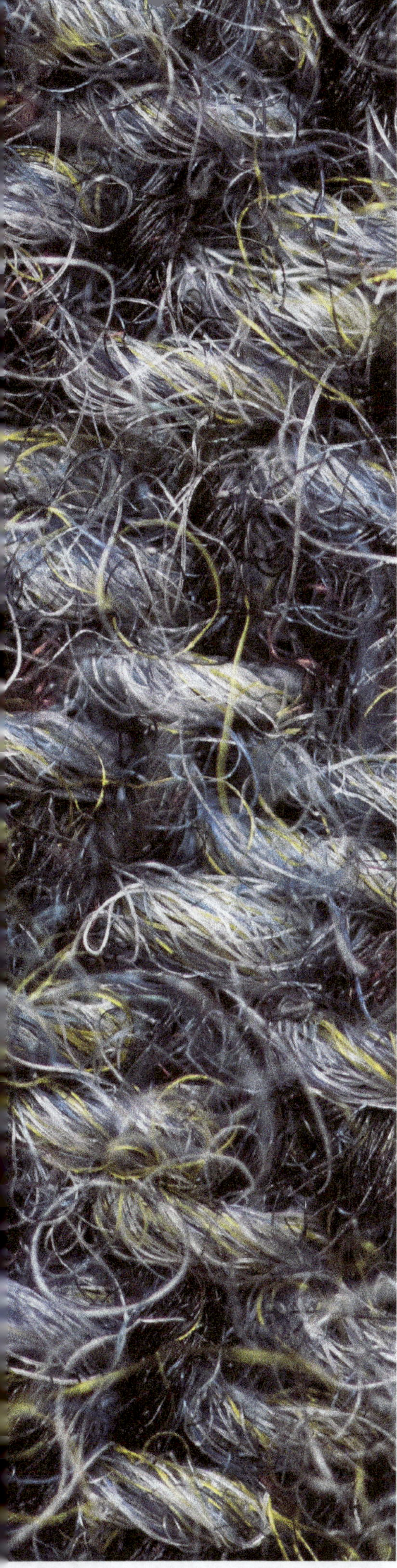

- Glitter Duct Tape
- Glitter Iron-On
- Glitter Vinyl
- Gossamer
- Grocery Bag
- Grois Point
- Grosgrain
- Habutai
- Handmade Paper
- Heat Transfer
- Heather
- Heavy Chipboard 2.0 mm
- Heavy Fabrics (e.g., denim)
- Bonded Heavy Fabrics (e.g., denim)
- Heavy Patterned Paper
- Heavy Watercolor Paper – 140 lb
- Holographic Vinyl
- Homespun Fabric
- Interlock Knit
- Melton Wool
- Mesh
- Metallic Leather
- Microfiber
- More
- Monk's Cloth
- Mulberry Foil Paper
- Mulberry Paper

REC

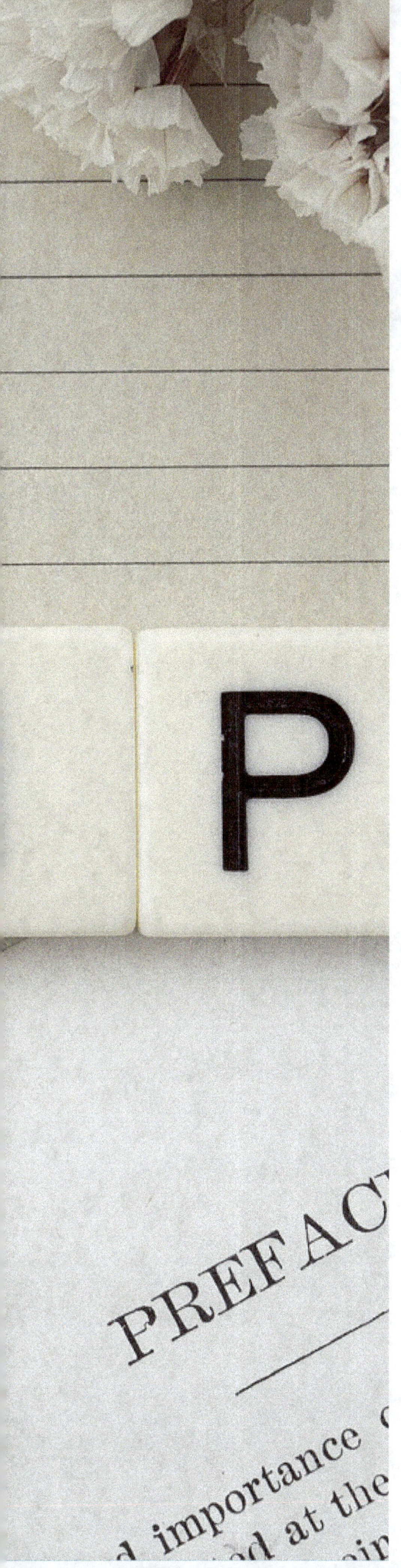

Chapter 2

Paper and cardstock projects

RECIPE STICKERS

MATERIALS NEEDED

-Cricut' cutting machine,
-Sticker paper
-Cutting mat.

DIRECTION

Use your "Cricut ID" to log in to the "Design Space" application. Then click on the "New Project" button on the top right corner of the screen to start a new project and view a blank canvas.

Click on the "Images" icon on the "Design Panel" and type in "recipe stickers" in the search bar. Select the image that works for you, then click on the "Insert Images" button at the bottom of the screen, as shown in the picture below.

The image that you have selected will appear on the canvas and can be edited to your preference. You will be able to make all kinds of changes, for example, changing the color and size of the image (sticker should be between 2-4 inches wide). The image selected for this project has the words 'stickers' inside the design, so let's delete that by first clicking on the "Ungroup" button and selecting the "Stickers" layer, and clicking on the red "x" button. Click on the "Text" button and add your recipe's name, as shown in the picture below.

Now, move the text to the middle of the design and select the entire design, including the reader. Then click on "Align" and select "Center Horizontally" and "Center Vertically" so that your text will be uniformly aligned right in the center of the design. Select all the design layers and click on the "Group" icon on the top right of the screen under "Layers Panel." Now, copy and paste the designs, update the text for all your recipes, as shown in the picture below. (Tip - You can use your keyboard shortcuts like "Ctrl + C" (to copy) and "Ctrl + V" (to paste) instead of selecting the image and clicking on "Edit" from the "Edit bar" to view the dropdown option for "Copy" and "Paste.")

Click on "Save" at the top right corner of the screen and enter a name for your project, for example, "Recipe Stickers," then click "Save," as shown in the picture below.

Your design is ready to be cut. Simply click on the "Make It" button on the top right corner of the screen. All the required mats and materials will be displayed on the screen. (Tip: You can move your design on the carpet by simply dragging and dropping it anywhere on the mat to resemble the cutting space for your material on the actual cutting mat).

Once you have loaded the sticker paper to your "Cricut" cutting machine, click "Continue" at the bottom right corner of the screen to start cutting your design.

Once your "Cricut" device has been connected to

RECIPE

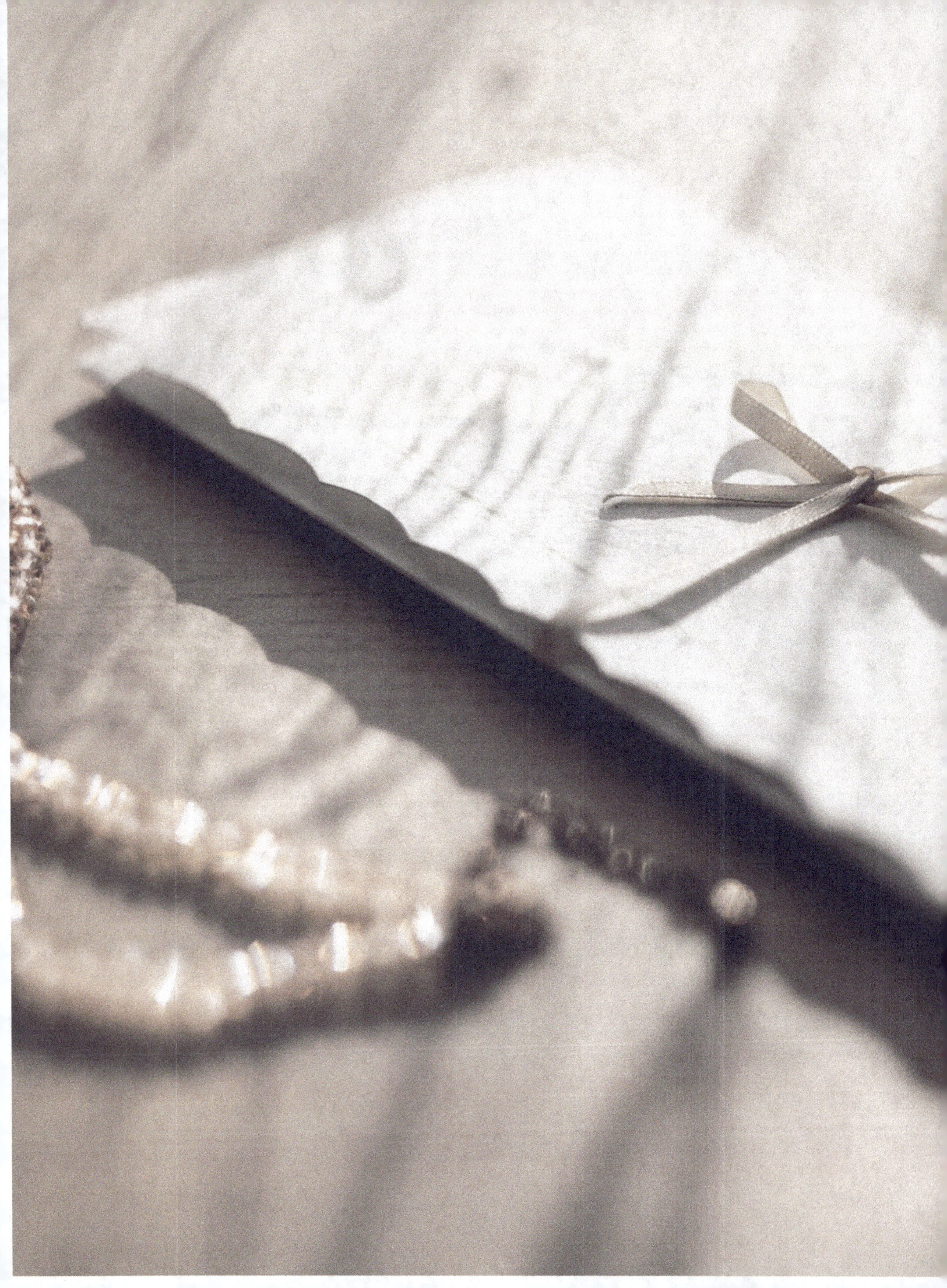

your computer, set the cut setting to "Vinyl" (recommended to cut the sticker paper since it tends to be thicker than regular paper). Place the sticker paper on top of the cutting mat and load it into the "Cricut" device by pushing it against the rollers. The "Load/Unload" button would already be flashing, so just press that button first, followed by the flashing "Go" button. Viola! You have newly created your very own recipe stickers.

WEDDING INVITATIONS

MATERIALS NEEDED

-"Cricut" cutting machine,
-Cutting mat,
-Cardstock
-Decorative paper/crepe paper/fabric, home printer
 (if not using "Cricut Maker").

DIRECTION

Use your "Cricut ID" to log in to the "Design Space" application. Then click on the "New Project" button on the top right corner of the screen to start a new project and view a blank canvas.
A beginner-friendly way to create wedding invitations is to customize an already existing project from the "Design Space" library that aligns with your ideas. Click on the "Projects" icon on the "Design Panel," then select "Cards" from the "All Categories" dropdown. Enter the
You can click on the project to preview its description and requirements. Once you have found the

project you want to use, click "Customize" at the bottom of the screen to edit the invite and add the required text to it.

The design will be loaded onto the canvas. Click on the "Text" button and type in the details for your invite. You will modify the font, color, and alignment of the text from the "Edit Text Bar" on top of the screen. You can even adjust the size of the entire design as needed. (An invitation card can be anywhere from 6 to 9 inches wide) Select the entire design and click on the "Group" icon on the screen's top-right under "Layers Panel." Then click on the "Save" button to enter a name for your project and click "Save" again.

Your design can now be printed then cut. Simply click on the "Make It" button on the top right corner of the screen to view the required mats and material. Then use your home printer to print the design on your chosen fabric (white cardstock or paper), or if using the "Cricut Maker," then just follow the prompts on the "Design Space" application. Load the material with printed design to your "Cricut" cutting machine and click "Continue" at the bottom right corner of the screen to start cutting your design.

Once your "Cricut" device has been connected to your computer, set the cut setting to "cardstock." Then place the printed cardstock on top of the cutting mat and load it into the "Cricut" device by pushing against the rollers. The "Load/Unload" button would already be flashing, so just press that button first, followed by the flashing "Go" button. Viola! You have your wedding invitations all ready to be put in an envelope on their way to your wedding guests.

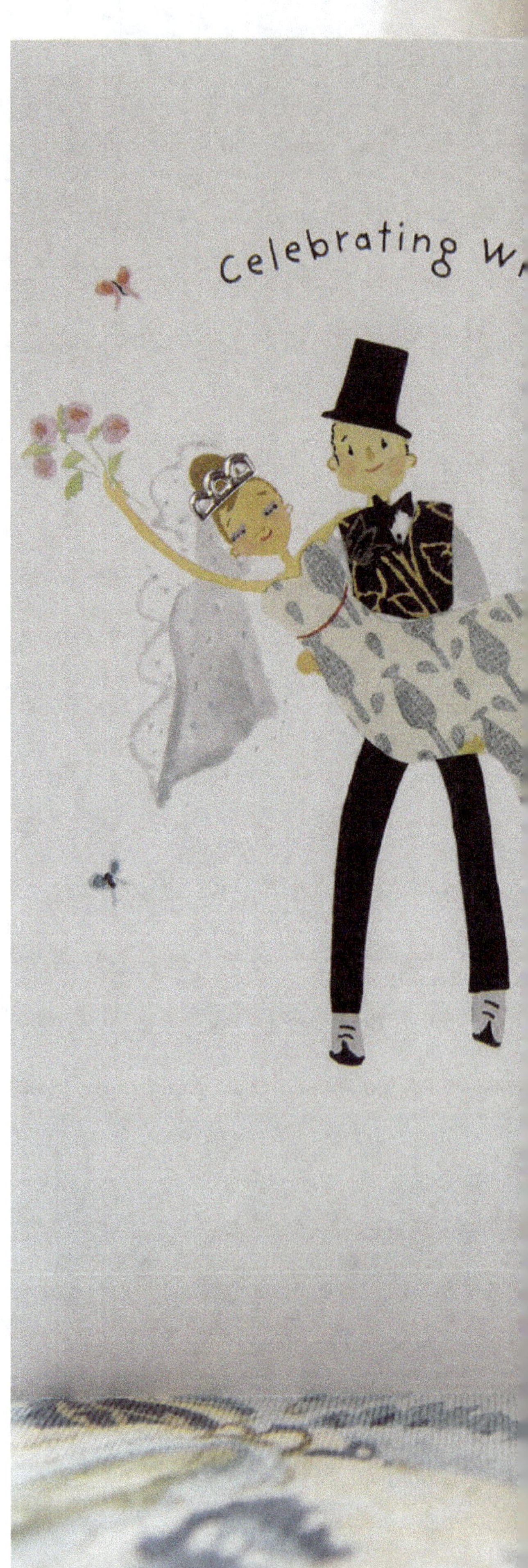

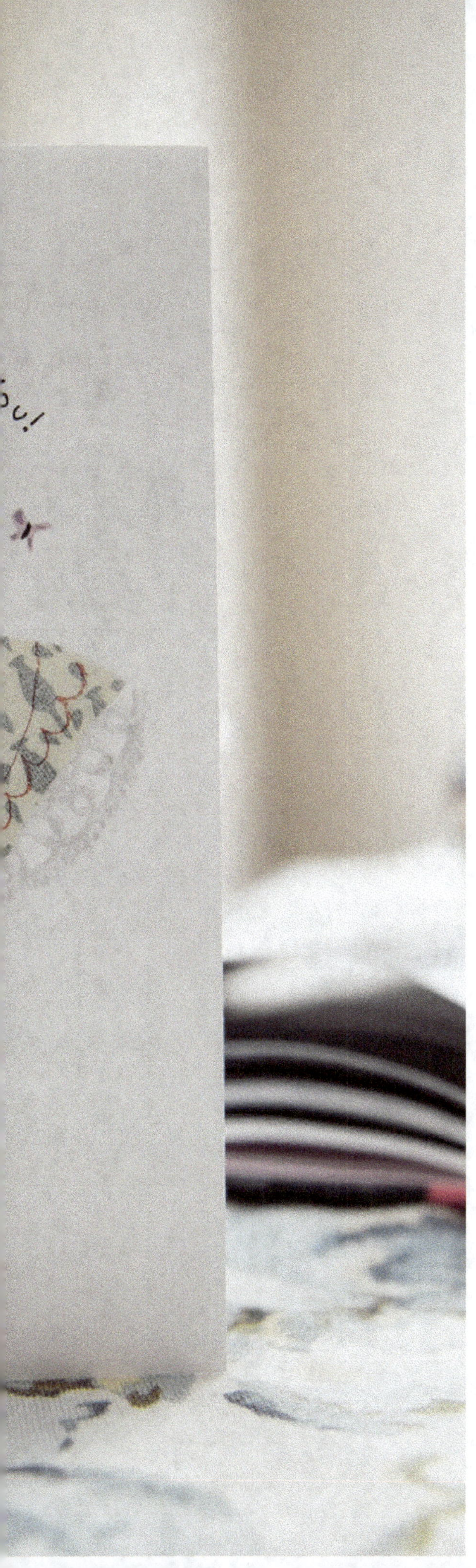

CUSTOM NOTEBOOKS

MATERIALS NEEDED

-"Cricut" cutting machine,
-Cutting mat,
-Washi sheets
-Decorative paper/crepe paper/fabric.

DIRECTION

Use your "Cricut ID" to log in to the "Design Space" application. Then click on the "New Project" button on the top right corner of the screen to start a new project and view a blank canvas.

Let's use an already existing project from the "Cricut" library for this. Click on the "Projects" icon on the "Design Panel" and type in "notebook" in the search bar.

You can view all the projects available by clicking on them, and a pop-up window displaying all the details of the project will appear on your screen. Select the project you like and click on "Customize" to edit this project to your preference further. The selected project will be displayed on the Canvas. You can check from the "Layers Panel" if your design contains only one layer, which is very easy to modify, or multiple layers that can be selectively adjusted. Click on the "Linetype Swatch" to view the color palette and select the desired color for your design.

Once you have modified the design to your satisfaction, it is ready to be cut. Simply click on the "Make It" button on the top right corner of the screen to view the required mats and material

for your project.
Load the washi paper sheet to your "Cricut" cutting machine and click "Continue" at the bottom right corner of the screen to start cutting your design. Connect your "Cricut" device to your computer, place the washi paper or your chosen paper on top of the cutting mat and load it into the "Cricut" machine by pushing against the rollers. The "Load/Unload" button would already be flashing, so just press that button first, followed by the flashing "Go" button. Viola! Your kids can now enjoy their uniquely customized notebook.

PAPER FLOWERS

MATERIALS NEEDED

-"Cricut" cutting machine,
-Cutting mat, cardstock,
-Adhesive.

DIRECTION

Use your "Cricut ID" to log in to the "Design Space" application. Then click on the "New Project" button on the top right corner of the screen to start a new project and view a blank canvas.
Click on the "Images" icon on the "Design Panel" and type in "flower" in the search bar. Then select the image you like and click on the "Insert Images" button at the bottom of the screen.

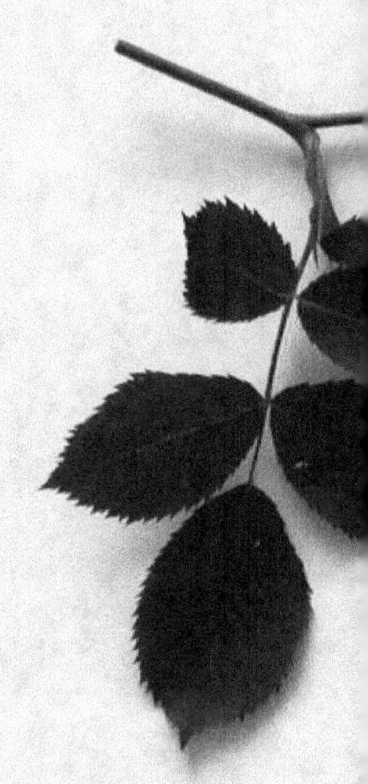

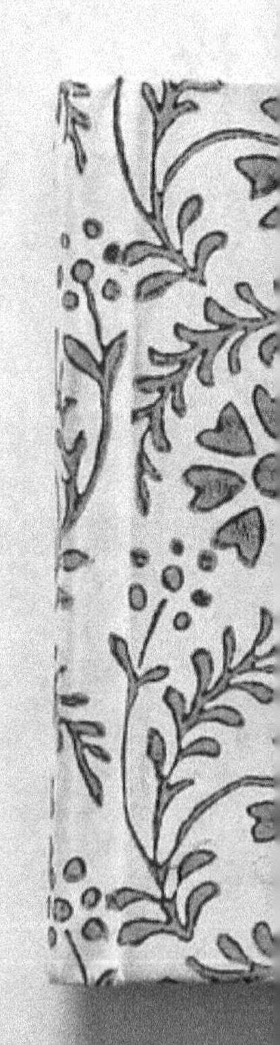

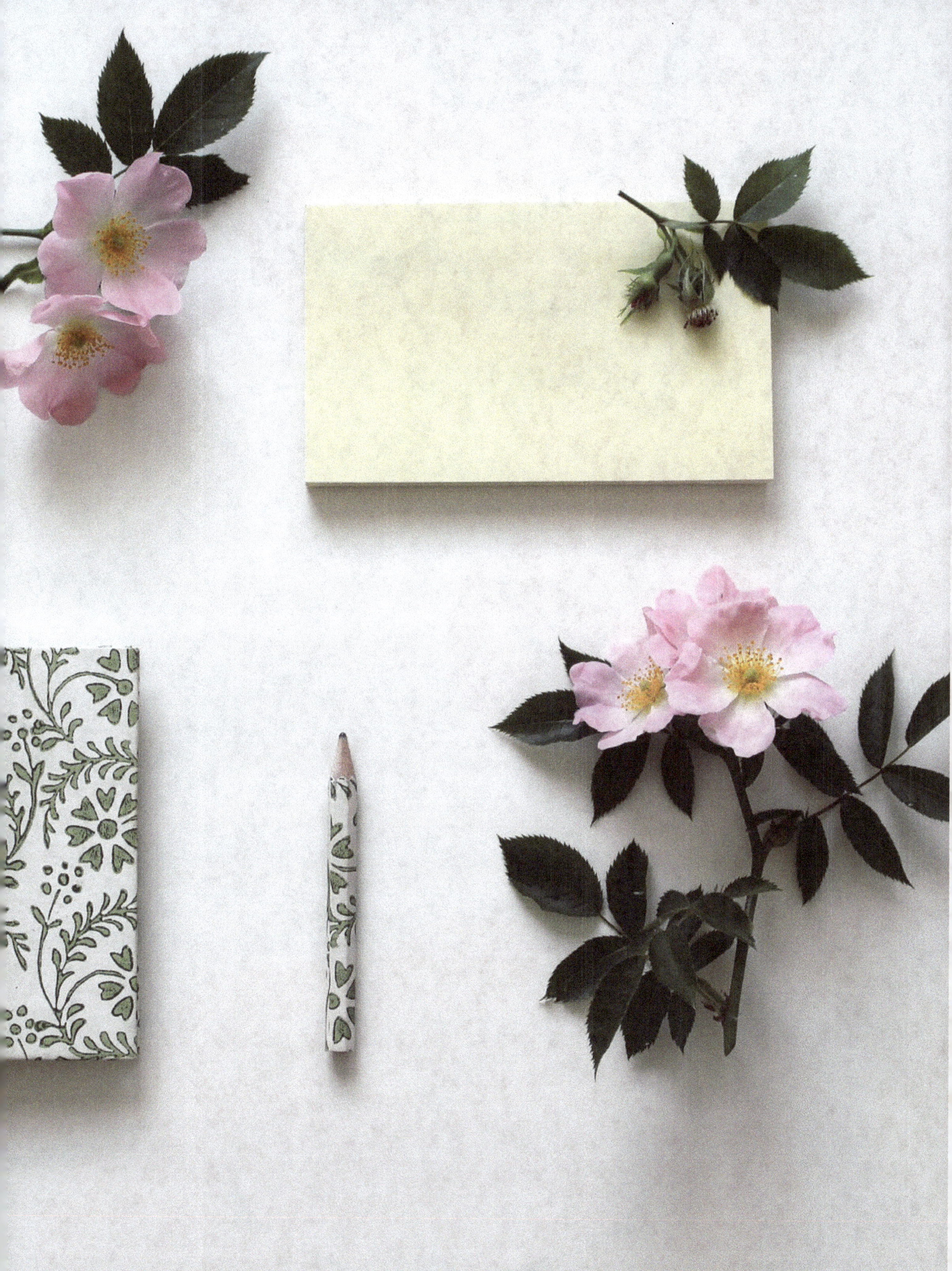

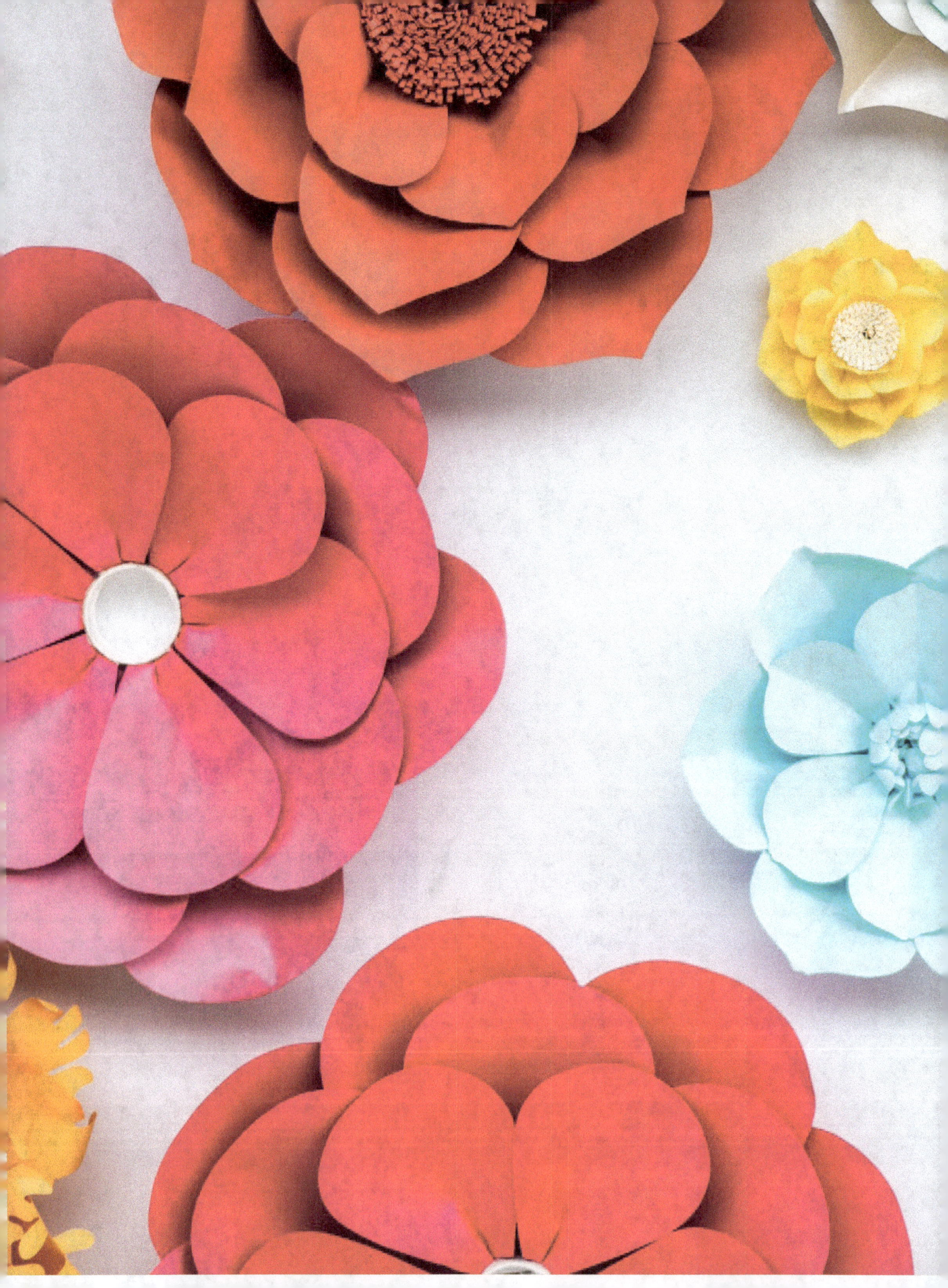

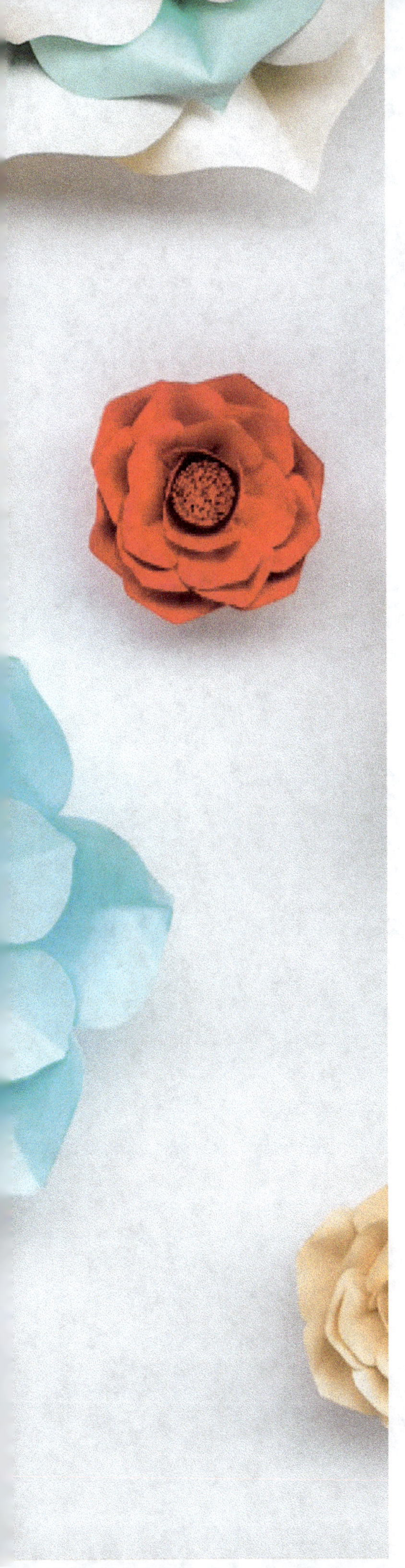

The selected image will be displayed on the canvas and edited using appropriate tools from the "Edit Image Bar." Then copy and paste the flower five times and make them a size smaller than the preceding height to create a variable length for depth and texture for the design. Click on the "Linetype Swatch" to view the color palette and select the desired color for your design.

Once you have modified the design to your satisfaction, it is ready to be cut. Simply click on the "Make It" button on the top right corner of the screen to view the required mats and material for your project.

Load the cardstock to your "Cricut" cutting machine and click "Continue" at the bottom right corner of the screen to start cutting your design.

Connect your "Cricut" device to your computer, place the cardstock or your chosen paper on top of the cutting mat, load it into the "Cricut" machine by pushing against the rollers. The "Load/Unload" button would already be flashing, so just press that button first, followed by the flashing "Go" button.

Once the design has been cut, simply remove the cut flowers and bend them at the center. Then using the adhesive, stack the flowers with the most considerable height at the bottom.

FRUITY TRAY

MATERIAL NEEDED

-An octagonal tray, creating coral, light yellow, white, and leaf green decorative paints.
-One or two flat brushes
-A pencil
-A 10cm paper disc and brown
-Black and glitter green poses
-Polish glue to varnish spray and masking tape.

DIRECTION

Draw disks on your board and paint them green (mix leaf green with light yellow). It will be necessary to make two layers. After drying, make yellow ovals in the center (light yellow and white) and paint in two coats. All this can be done using the Cricut template

Trace the outlines of the discs in brown. Draw the green lines (see photo) in the green area and then the pips. Apply a spray varnish to prevent the posca from drooling in the glue varnish in the next step. Stick the stickers with the varnish glue at the bottom of the tray. After drying, apply a little varnish in spray to prevent the stickers' ink from dissolving in contact with the resin.

Using a glue gun, attach the small wooden fruit decorations.

First of all, the tray's bottom must be varnished to prevent inks/colors/paints from bleeding into the paint. It is not systematic, but it could happen, so you better take the lead.

Then, respect the dosages of the packaging and

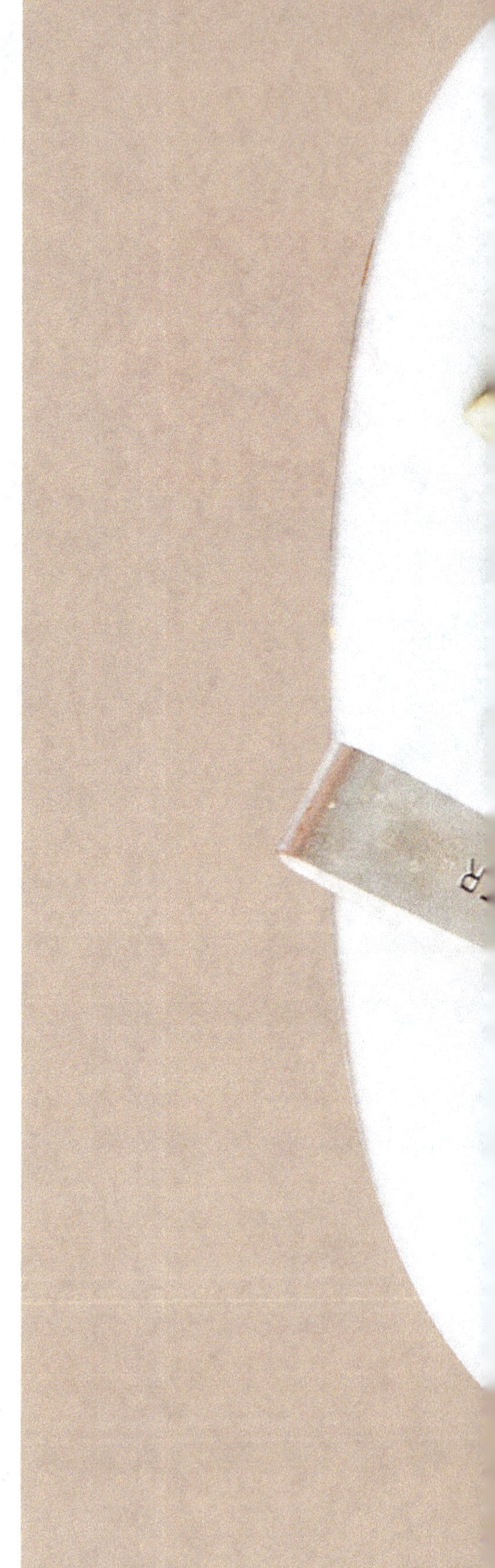

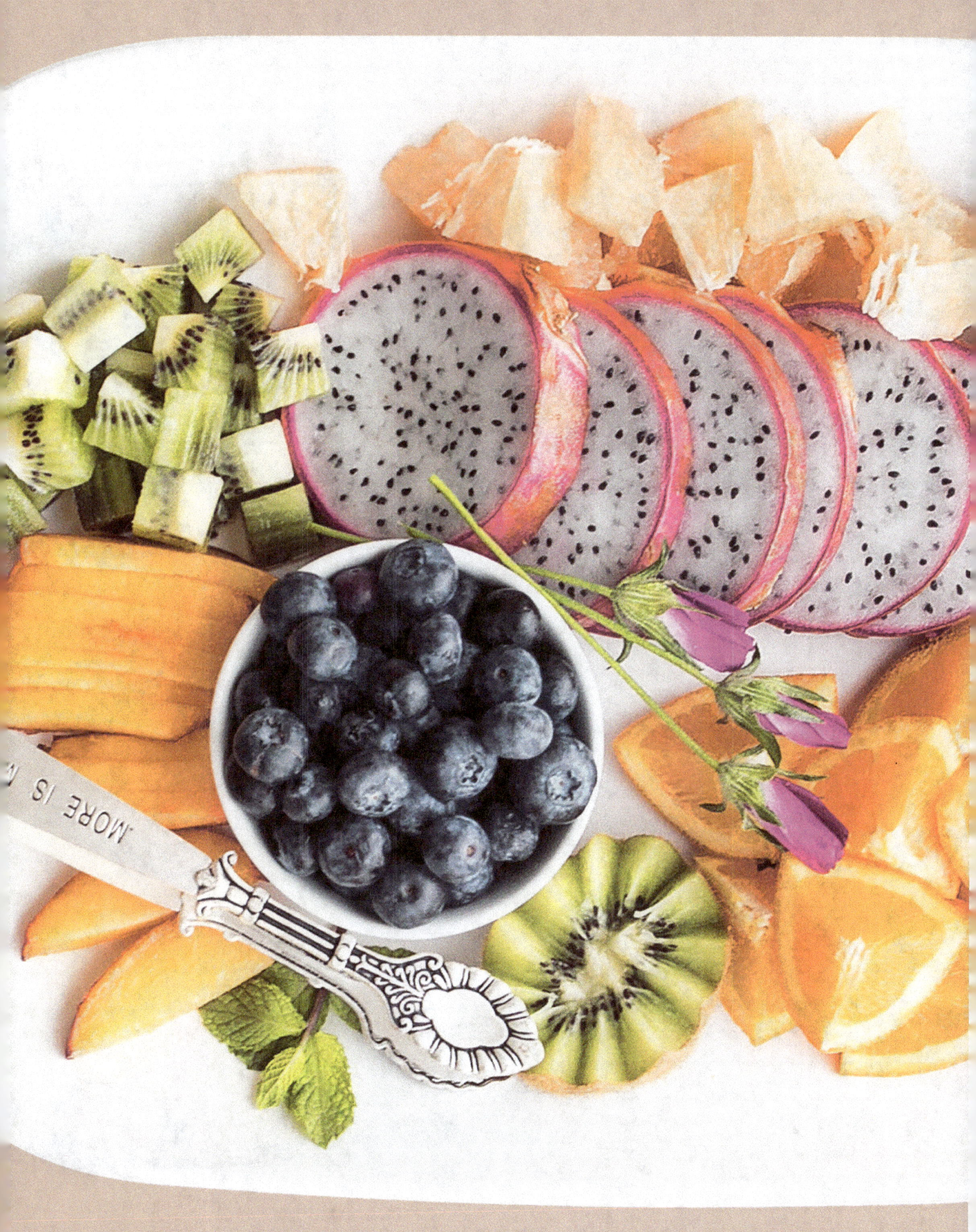
MORE IS M

check that you pour the hardener first. - Mix for a long time. Ten minutes minimum per cup. Here there are two cups I have mixed over 20 minutes. Don't hesitate to transfer your mixture to a new cup and mix again. - pour the resin in the center of the tray and distribute the whole by tilting it. Let dry for two days, even if the packaging says 24h.

CRAFT PAPER PENCIL HOLDER

MATERIALS NEEDED

-Imitation leather kraft paper braiding tape - 9.5 cm
-Self-healing cutting mat - 60x45 cm
-Transparent ruler for creative hobbies 40 cm
-Scissors
-Mini high-temperature glue gun
-Pencil
-Salvaged cardboard, glass, and jar or compass

DIRECTION

Take a glass and a jar with different diameters. Trace the outlines of the circles on recycled cardboard and cut them. In addition to this, you need to know more about it.
Glue the cardboard discs together with the glue gun. Cut strips of kraft paper braiding 20 cm long. Glue them one by one in radiation. Superimpose them slightly at the base: the bands must be edge at the cardboard disc's circumference. In addition to this, you need to know more about it.
Cover the larger cardboard disc in this way. Glue

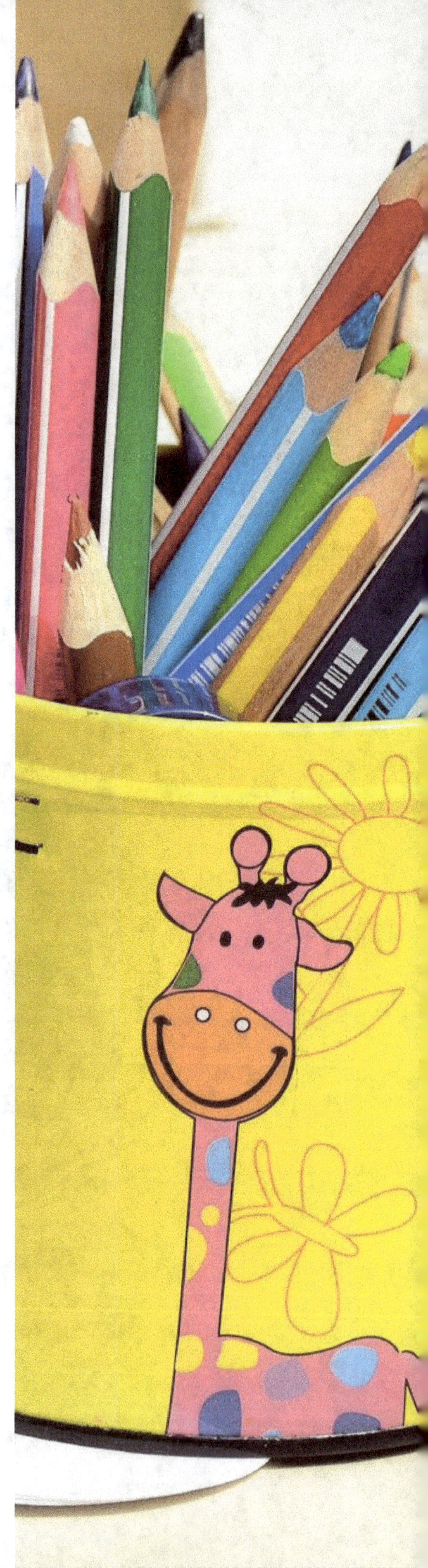

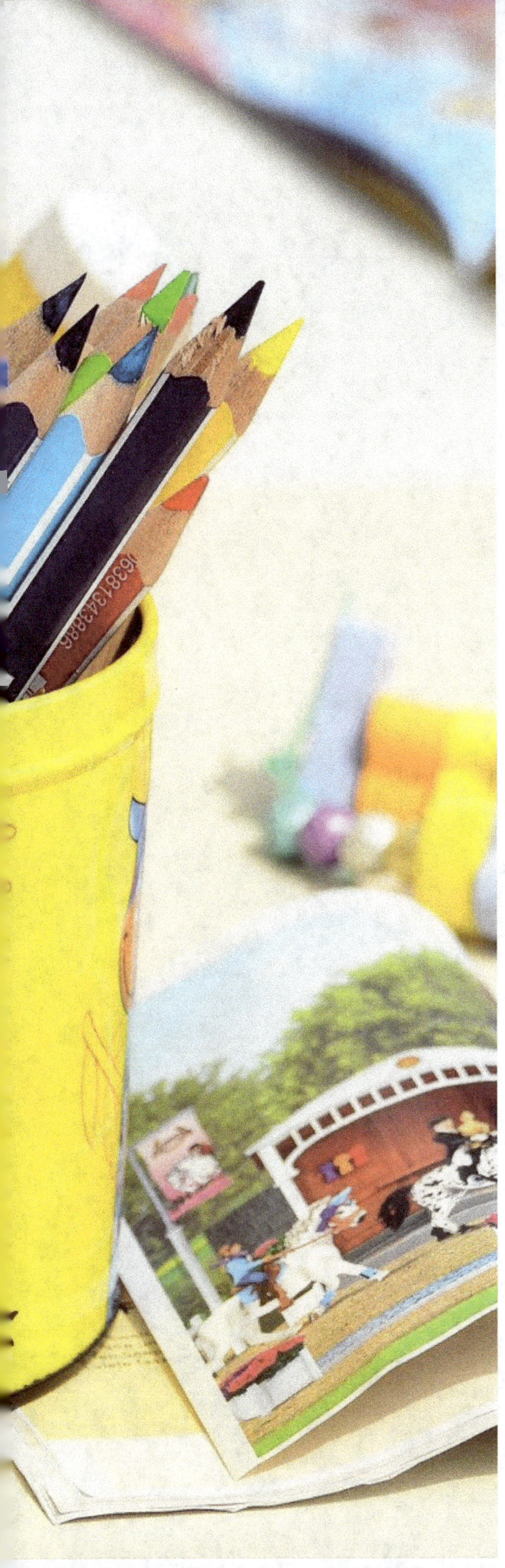

with a glue gun. Fold the braiding strips, measure the cardboard disc's circumference, and cut five braiding strips of this size. In addition to this, you need to know more about it.

Slide a strip of braiding perpendicular under one of those welded to the cardboard base. Stick one end to it, as close as possible to the ground. Pass it alternately under one vertical strip and over the next one. Attach a dot of glue to the glue gun under a few vertical stripes.

To close, glue the second end of the strip under the first end. In the same way, slip the second strip of braiding, mount a double row, tightening to avoid gaping spaces.

Set up the braiding of the pot with five strips in all. Fold a base strip towards the inside of the pool. Mark the fold in the pot to mark the length. Cut off the excess. In addition to this, you need to know more about it.

Cut a strip of braiding a little larger than the circumference of the pot. Glue to the top edge of the pot with a glue gun. Fold the strips one by one towards the inside of the pot. Glue them with a glue gun. R with a glue gun.9. The pot is ready to accommodate the pencils in your office.

BIRTH ANNOUNCEMENT CARD

MATERIALS NEEDED

-An assortment of Parisian ties "newborn girl."
-An assortment of 80 Parisian ties - Pink
-Alphabet Glitter uppercase - Pink

-25 Pollen folded cards 135x135 mm - White
-Mahé sheet 30.5 x 30.5 cm white
-Mahé sheet 30.5 x 30.5 cm pale pink
-Tube of universal gel glue - Cultura - 30 ml
-Precision cutter and three blades
-Self-healing cutting mat - 30x22 cm
-An assortment of 3 precision tools
-Transparent ruler for creative hobbies 30 cm
-Template to download and print

DIRECTION

To start, download, print, and reproduce the heart template. Hollow out the pattern using the cutter to create a stencil.
Cut an 11 x 11 cm pink square and a 10.5 x 10.5 cm white square.
Center the stencil on the white paper square and secure it with adhesive paper to prevent it from moving.
Place a few Parisian ties to guide you in their positioning inside the cutout heart.
Using a precision cutter or paper punch, pierce your card and insert the Parisian clips.
Once the heart is filled, glue the white part on the rose.
Finish by pasting the desired text (first name ..) to finalize the card.
The invitation is ready.

DIY BOOKMARK CAT —PAGE

MATERIALS

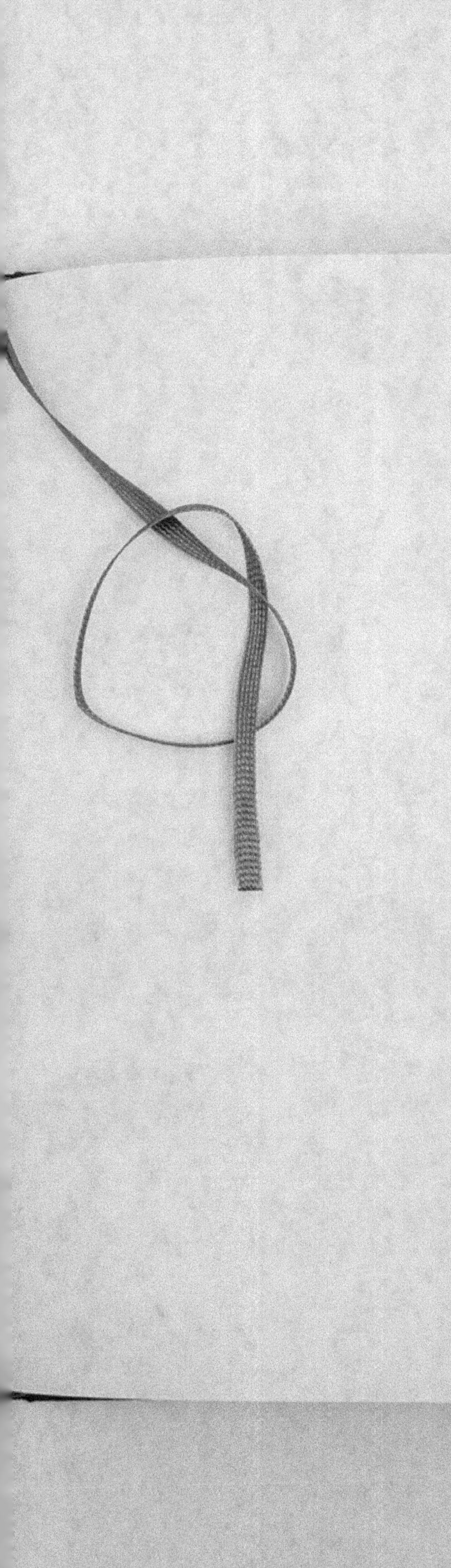

-Block of 20 multi-colored postcards sheets
-Glue
-Pouch of 24 decorated colored pencils
-6 round movable eyes Ø 12mm
-PERFO ROUND CLAMP 6MM
-5m roll of Glitter masking tape - Green
-5m roll of Glitter masking tape - White

DIRECTION

Print the template and choose its paper colors.
Cut out the template along the lines.
Copy the body's drawing, front legs, and back legs on the brown sheet, do the same in the purple sheet for the belly, and cut out.
Glue the elements together with glue.
To facilitate the gluing put a little glue on a cardboard plate and use a brush to spread it. Then clean the brush with warm water and soap.
Glue the movable eyes, glue a piece of masking tape to make the collar, cut a piece of pink paper in a triangle for the nose, and draw the mouth, mustaches, and legs with a black pencil.
With the hole punch, make a small circle in the yellow paper and glue it to finalize the cat's collar.
To get an easy triangle nose, first cut out a square and cut it in half diagonally.
Write your name on the cat's belly with a colored pencil.
And there you have a lovely cat-page bookmark for your summer readings. I'm going to reread the adventures of the little wizard, and what will you read?
You can even do it in other colors so that it doesn't get boring!

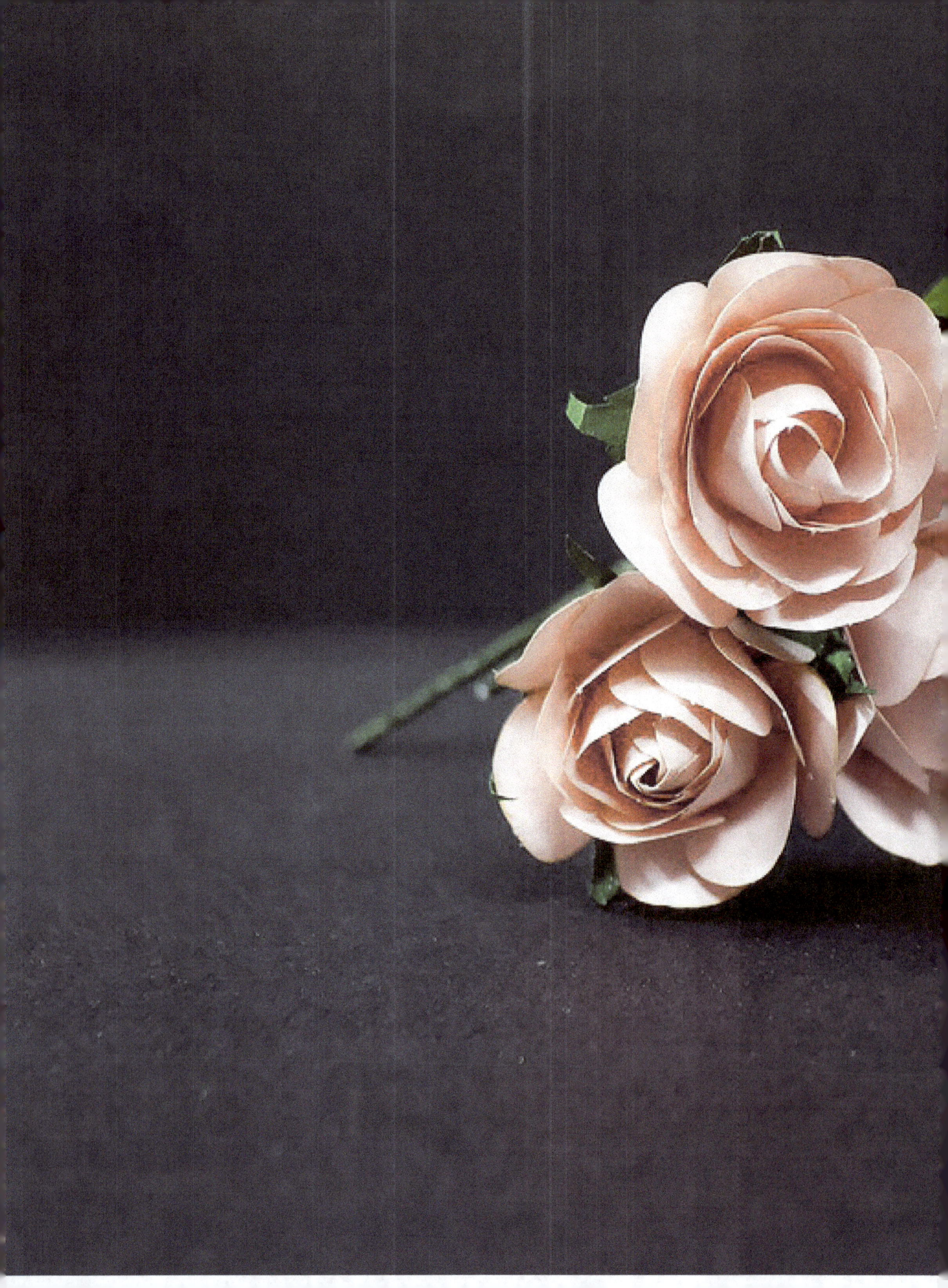

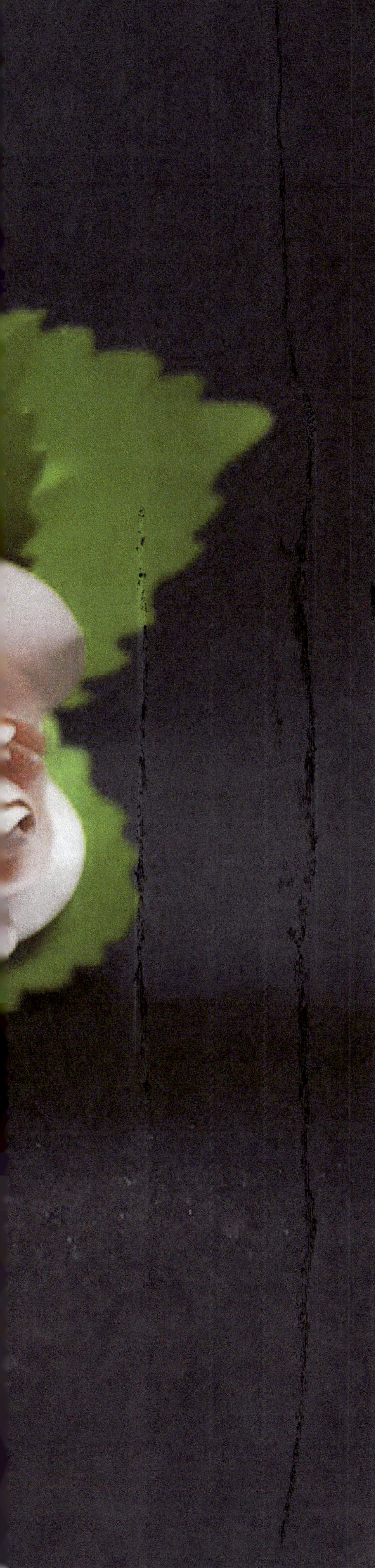

3D PAPER FLOWERS (PAPER)

MATERIALS NEEDED:

-Cricut Machine
-Cricut mat
-Colored scrapbook paper
-Hot glue gun and glue sticks

DIRECTION

To make flowers, you need an appropriate shape for the petals. To make such a shape, you can combine three ovals of equal size. To create an oval, select the circle tool and make a circle. Then click the unlock button at the bottom of the shape. Once this is done, you can reshape the circle to form an oval.

Duplicate this oval twice and rotate each duplicate a little, keeping the bottom at the same point, as shown in the picture.

Select all three ovals and weld them together to get your custom petal shape. For each large flower, you need 12 petals - each one about 3 inches long, while for each small flower, you need eight petals - each one about 2 inches long. For each flower, you need a circle shape for the base of about the same width as each petal. Arrange the petals and base circle shape in Cricut Design Studio.

Set your material to cardstock on Design Space or the machine, then cut the petals out depending on your machine.

After you cut out the petals, remove them and cut a slit about half an inch long in the bottom of each one. Place a bit of glue on the left side and glue the right side over each petal's glue.

The next thing to do is to place the petals on the circle base. For large flowers, you need three circles of four petals each. For small flowers, you need five circles on the outside and three on the inside. Put a bit of hot glue on the petal and add to the circle as described above.

For the center of the flowers, search Cricut Access for "flower" and chose shapes with several small petals. Cut these out using a different color of cardstock and glue to the center of the flowers.

LUMINARIES

MATERIALS NEEDED:

-Luminary Graphic (From a Cricut Project)
-Sugar Skull (SVG File)
-Cricut Explore Air or Cricut Maker
-Cardstock Sampler
-Scoring Stylus
-Glue Stick
-Battery-Operated Tea Light

DIRECTION

The first step is to open your Luminary graphic on the Design Space.

Then go ahead to upload the SVG file of your Sugar Skull and adjust its size to around 3.25" high. After doing that, move the Sugar Skull to the more significant part of the Luminary graphic (in the middle of the two score lines) and cen-

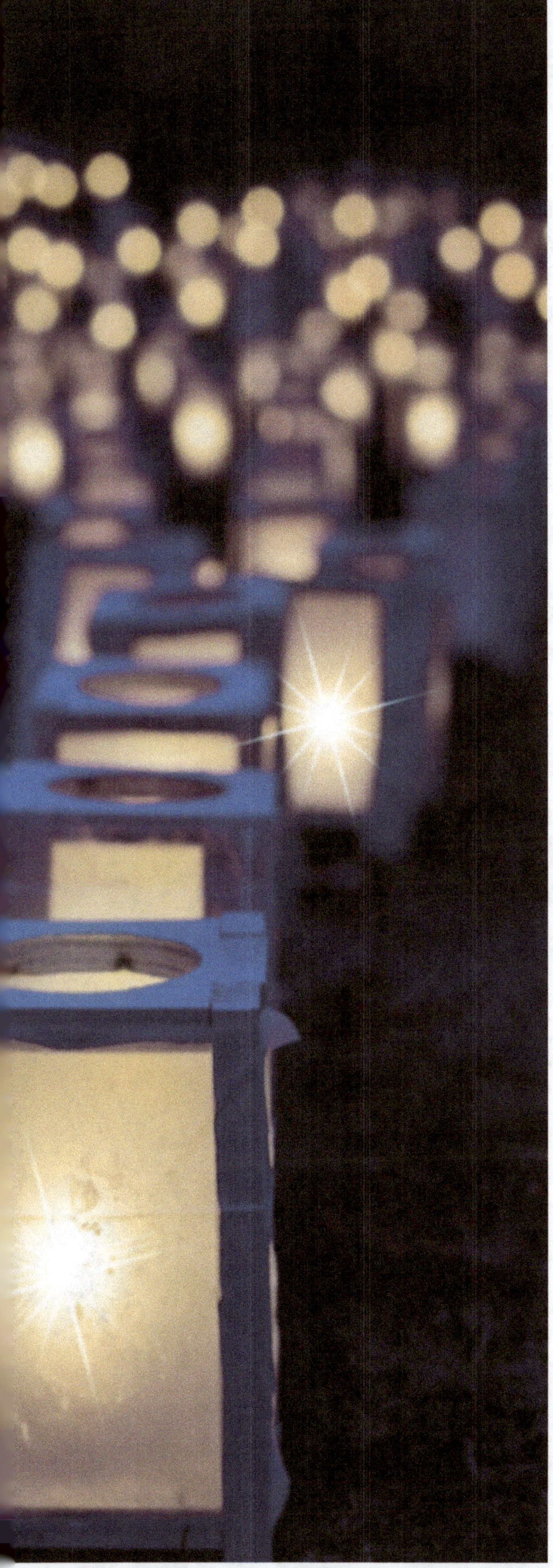

ter-align it.

Select the Sugar Skull and the Luminary Graphic and then go ahead and click on "Weld."

Try selecting every graphic on the design space and click on "Attach." Then copy and paste the selected graphics on the same page (duplication).

Select "Make It" at the top right-hand corner, and then ensure everything is positioned correctly. Click on

"Continue." If you notice the files being cut on two different mats, just move them back together on one single mat by merely clicking on these three dots located at the graphic corner.

Select "Light Cardstock" under the "Materials" menu, and then start loading the Mat and Cut. Also, ensure that your Scoring Stylus is in Clamp A. This will automatically change your machine settings from scoring to cutting.

When the cut-out is done, fold it along the Score lines. Then start gluing the small Flap to the interior part of the lantern's back.

Switch on the Battery-Operated Tea Light, and then place your lantern on top of it.

TABLE DECORATION

MATERIALS NEEDED

-Set of 6 Scrapbooking paper sheets - Tropical Paradise
-Mahé Leaf - 30.5x30.5cm - petrol blue .
-Mahé Leaf - 30.5x30.5cm - menthol green

-Mahé Leaf - 30.5x30.5cm - lime green
-Mahé Leaf - 30.5x30.5cm - spring green
-Slate scrapbooking sheet - Mahé - 30x30cm
-A sheet of 34 epoxy stickers - Tropical Paradise
-Eight card stock polaroid frames - Tropical Paradise
-An assortment of 40 die-cuts - Tropical Paradise
-100m two-tone spool - Sky blue
-16 mini clothespins 35 mm
-Vivaldi smooth sheet A4 240g - Canson - white
n ° 1
-Precision cutter and three blades
-Blue cutting mat - 2mm - A3
-Black acrylic and aluminum ruler 30cm
-Precision scissors 13.5cm blue bi-material rings
-3D adhesive squares
-Mahé Tools - Easy Mounter - scrapbooking
-Pack of 6 HB graphite pencils

DIRECTION

Gather the materials.
Using the template and a pencil, reproduce the palm tree on the papers in the collection.
Cut out with a cutter or scissors.
Assemble the trunk of the palm tree. Glue the foliage. Using the template, reproduce the cocktail support traces on thin cardboard, following the dimensions indicated. Cover it with the collection paper.
After having cut in the slate sheet: 1 x (8.5 x 8.5 cm), choose a Polaroid. Glue the slate sheet to the back of the Polaroid. Using a chalk pen, write "Cocktail of the day." Decorate with the stickers. Fold the support at the dotted lines.
Using the templates and a pencil, draw the leaves and flowers on the Mahé paper and the collection

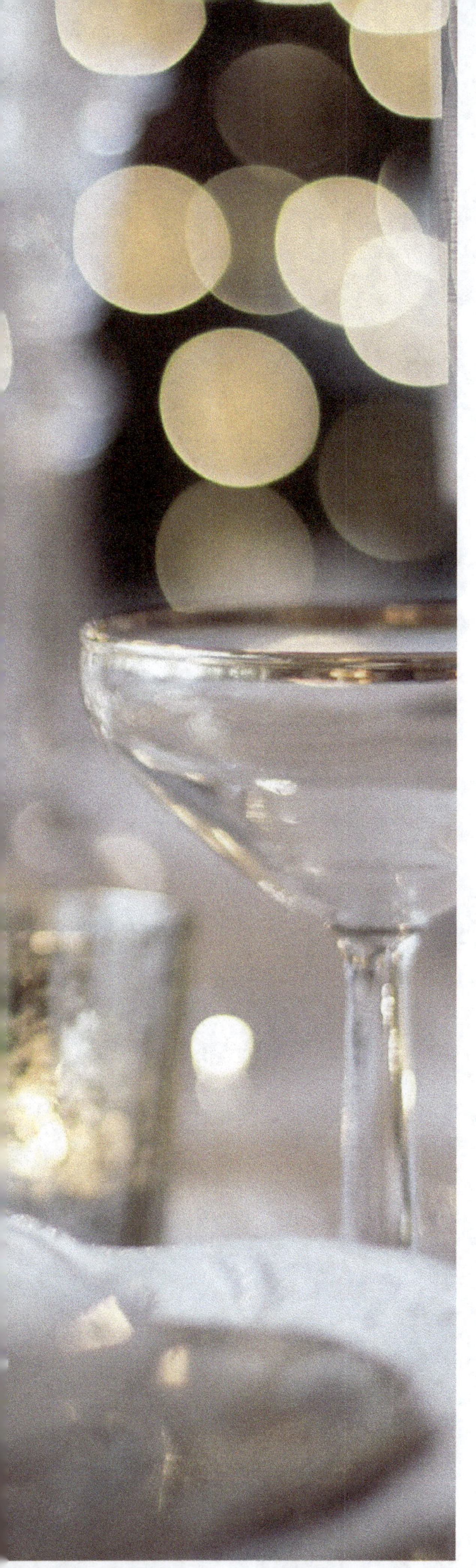

paper. Draw.

Choose photos. Cut them to size: 8.5 x 8.5 cm. Stick to the back of the Polaroids.

Glue the leaves and flowers together. Cut the string to the desired dimensions and glue it to the back of the flowers. Glue the birds on the string and hang the photos using mini clips.

And here is a pretty summer and tropical decoration! Beautiful evenings in perspective!

Chapter 3
Vinyl projects

VINYL CLOCK?

MATERIALS NEEDED

-Vinyl record
-Old Clock machine

DIRECTIONS

It can be implicated in so many ways. First of all, cut the vinyl record in a shape of your choice, square, triangle, flower, circle, and any shape.
Set the clock machine in the center of a vinyl record.
Use glue to fix it right in the center.
The vinyl clock is just ready for use. Place it on your desk by attaching some stand to it or hang it on your wall.

APRIL FOOLS GAG GLASS DECAL

MATERIALS NEEDED:

-Cricut Maker or Cricut Explore
-Standard Grip mat
-Black window cling

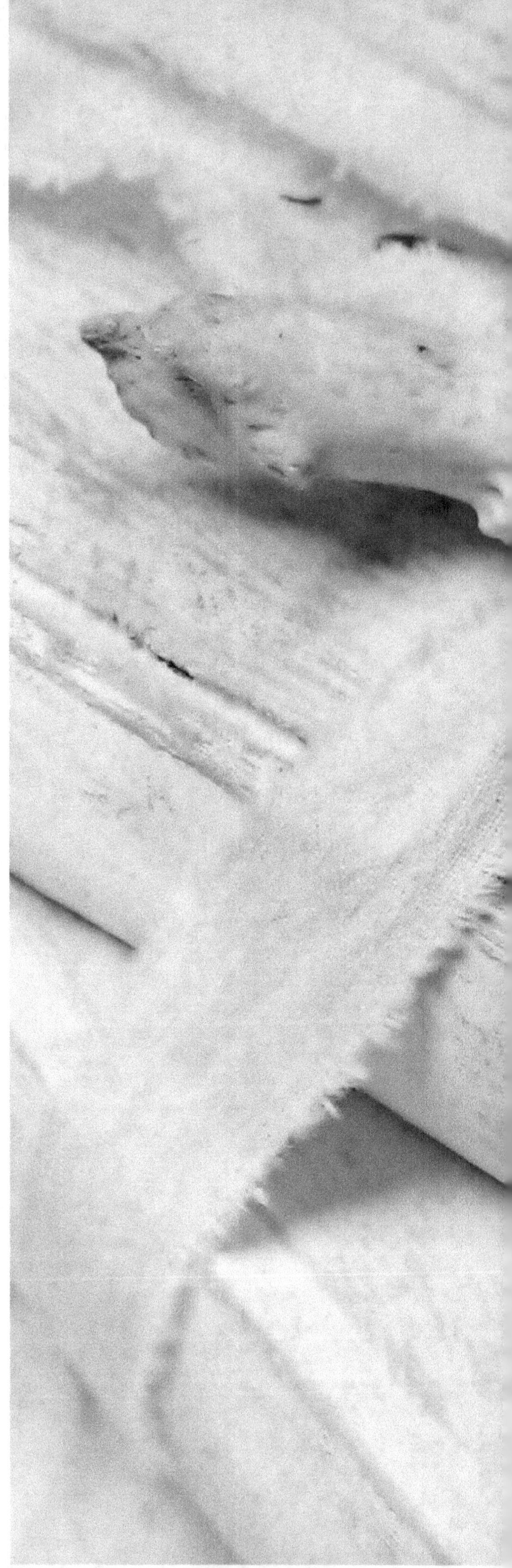

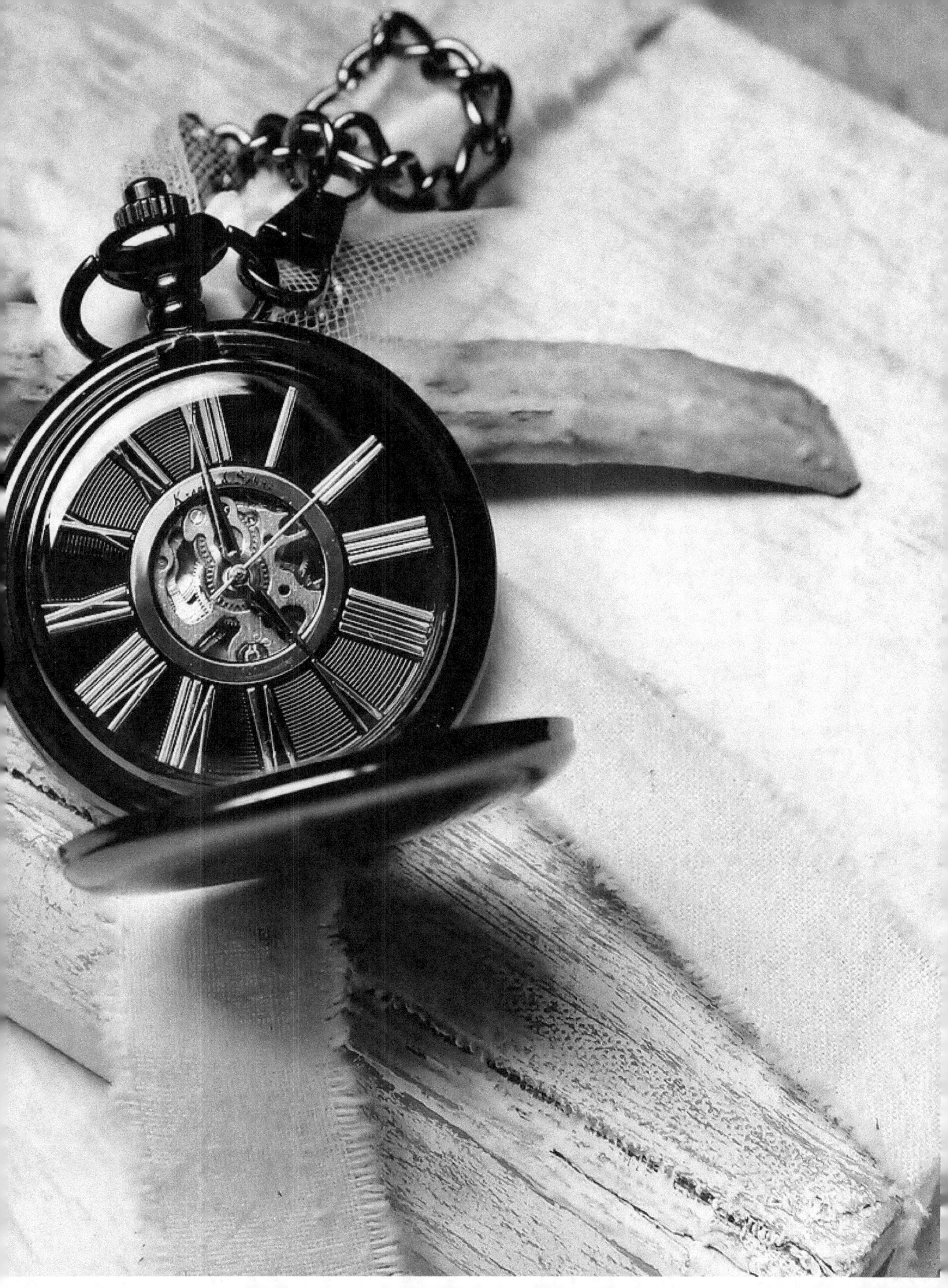

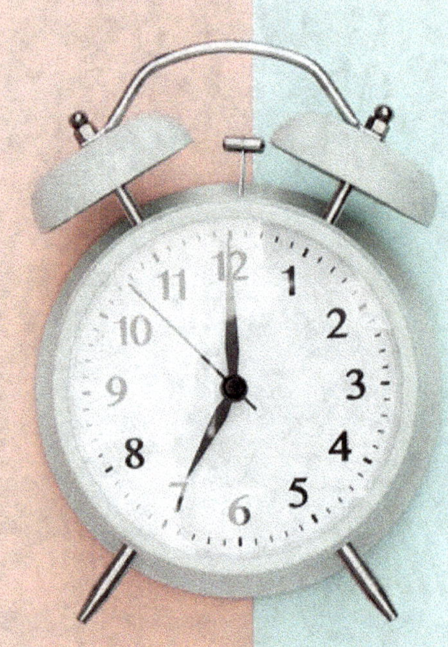

-Scraper
-Weeder
-Tall glass

DIRECTION

Log into the 'Design Space' application and click on the 'New Project' button on the screen's top right corner to view a blank canvas. Let us use text for this project. Click on 'Text' from the 'Designs Panel' on the left of the screen and type in 'You have been POISO-NED' or any other phrase that you may like. The font 'Chloe-Whimsy' was selected for the image below, as shown in the picture below. But you can let your creativity take over this step and choose any color or font that you like, making sure that the size of the design aligns with the size of the bottom of your glass. Select and copy-paste your image for the number of times you want to print your design.

Click on 'Save' to save the project, click on the 'Make It' button, load the window cling to your Cricut machine, and follow the Direction on the screen to cut the design.

Carefully remove the excess vinyl from the sheet.

To easily paste your design on the glass without stretching the pieces, put the transfer tape on top of the cut design.

After cleaning the surface, slowly peel the paper backing on the vinyl from one end to the other in a rolling motion to ensure even placement. Now, use the scraper tool on top of the transfer tape to remove any bubbles, and then just peel off the transfer tape.

SNOWMAN LANTERN

MATERIALS NEEDED:

-Cricut Maker or Cricut Explore
-Standard Grip mat
-Vinyl in desired colors
-Transfer tape
-Scraper
-Weeder
-Glass etching cream
-Glass faced lantern

DIRECTION

Log into the 'Design Space' application and click on the 'New Project' button on the screen's top right corner to view a blank canvas.
Click on the 'Projects' icon and type in 'Snowman Lantern' in the search bar.
Click on 'Customize' to edit the project to your preference further, click on the 'Make It' button, load the vinyl sheet to your Cricut machine, and follow the Direction the screen to cut your project.
Using a weeder tool, remove the negative space pieces of the design.
Use the transfer tape to apply the vinyl cuts to the glass face of the lantern.
Then use the scraper tool on top of the transfer tape to remove any bubbles, and then just peel off the transfer tape.

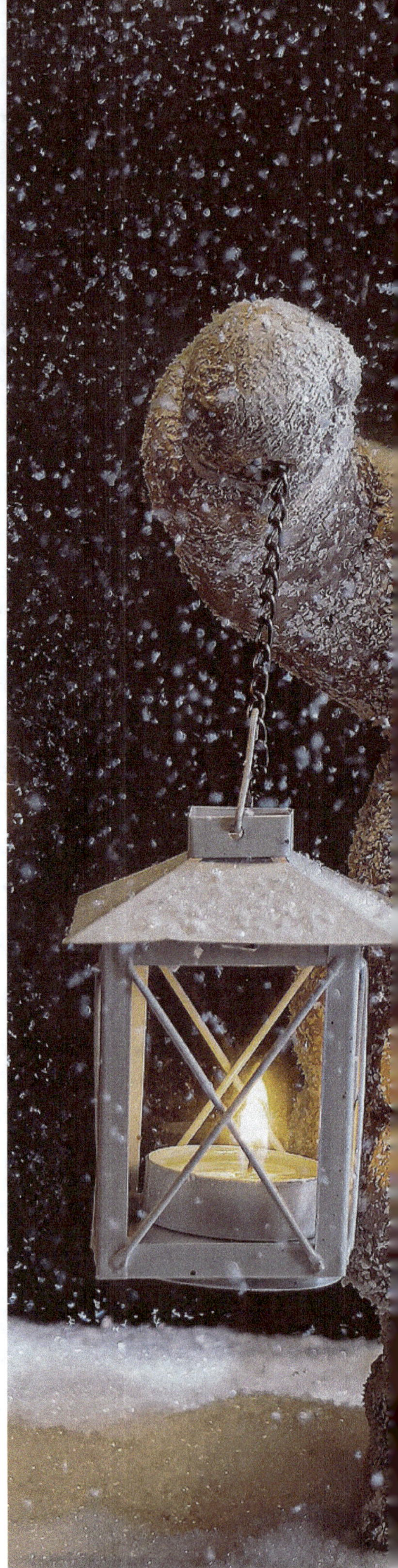

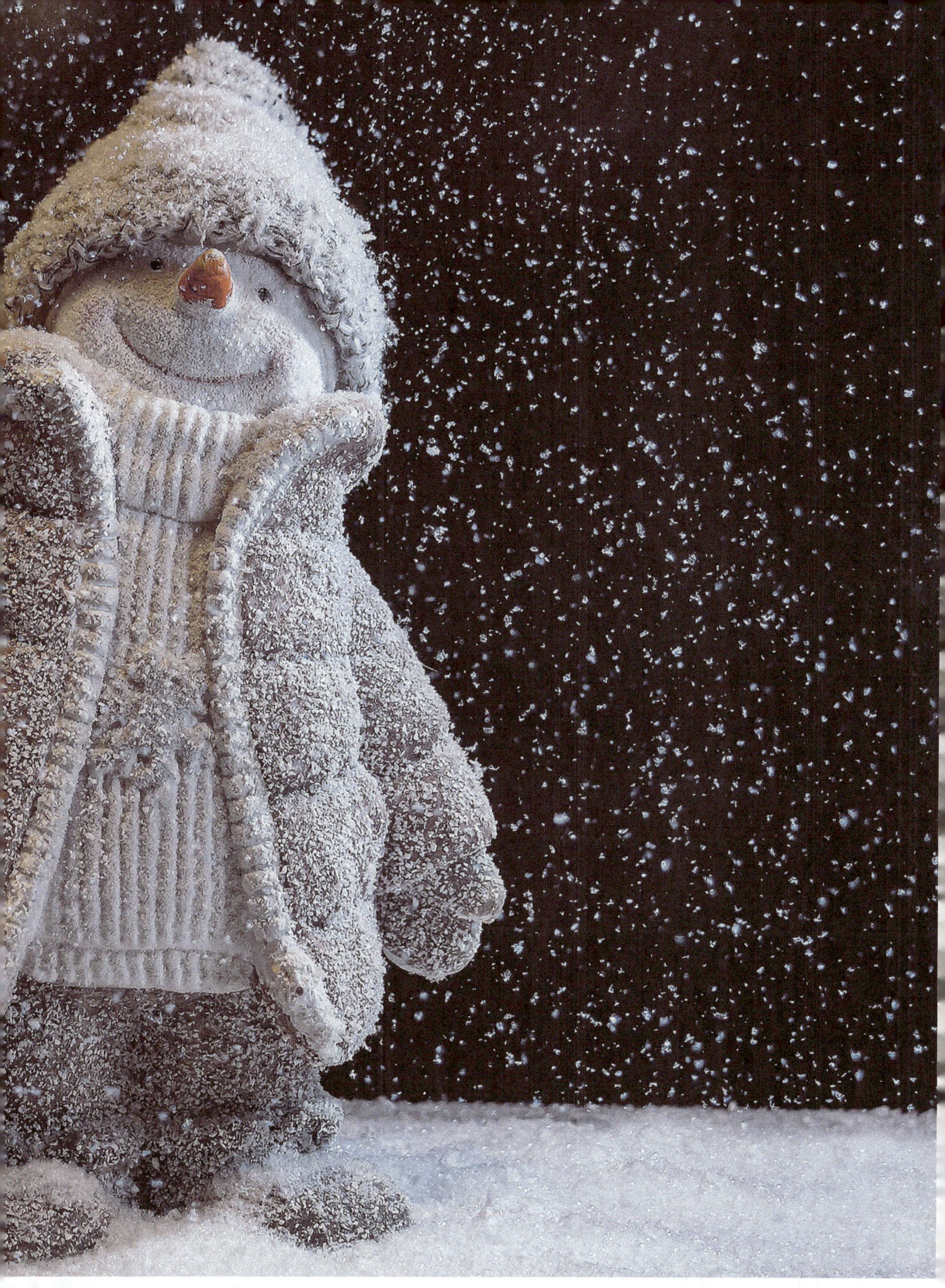

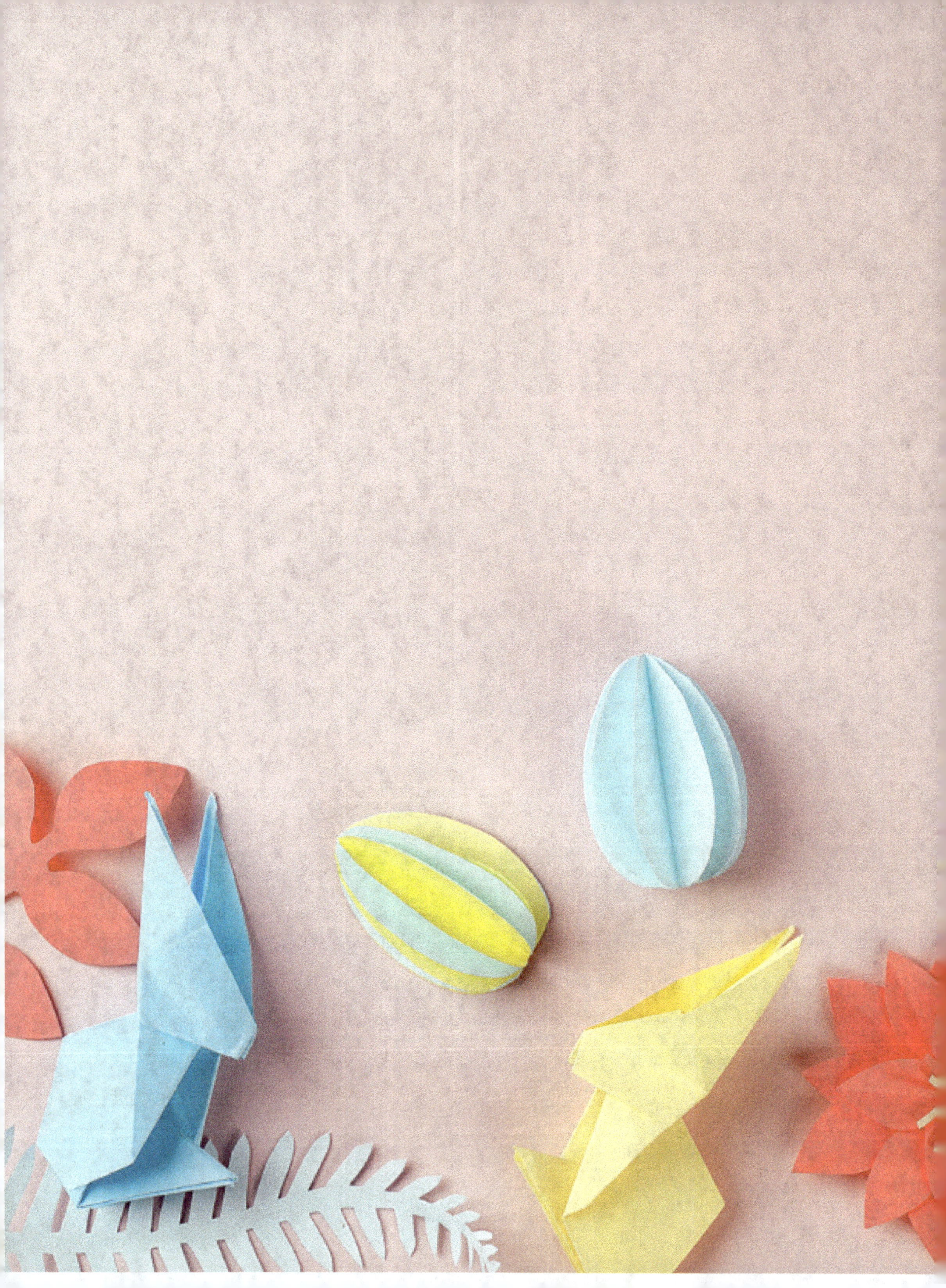

Lastly, apply the etching cream following the Direction package and rinse off to remove the vinyl.

PERSONALIZED COASTER TILES

MATERIALS NEEDED:

-Cricut Maker, or Cricut Explore
-Standard grip mat
-Printable Cricut iron-on or heat transfer vinyl
-Cricut Easy Press Mini Easy Press mat
-Weeding tool
-Ceramic coaster tiles

DIRECTION

Log in to the Design Space application, and click on the 'New Project' button on the screen's top right corner to view a blank canvas.

Let us use our image for this project. Search the web to find a monogram image that you would like and store it on your computer.

Now, click on the 'Upload' icon from the 'Designer Panel' on the screen's left.

A screen with 'Upload Image' and 'Upload Pattern' will be displayed.

Click on the 'Upload Image' button. Click on 'Browse,' or simply drag and drop your image on the screen.

Select the image type 'Simple' and save the image as a 'Print Then Cut Image.'

Choose the uploaded image by clicking on the 'Insert Images' and edit the image as needed.

You can personalize the monogram by adding text

to the design by clicking on the 'Text' icon and typing in 'Your Name' or any other phrase.

The font 'American Uncial Corn Regular' in regular and color (green) was selected for the image below.

Select the text and the image, click on 'Group,' copy-paste your design as many times as needed and save the project.

You can resize the design as needed to match your coaster's size, although the recommended size is 4 x 4 inches for most common tile coasters. The design is ready to be printed and cut. Simply click on the 'Make It' button and follow the screen prompts for using an ink jet printer to print the design on your printable iron-on vinyl and subsequently cut the design.

Carefully remove the excess material from the sheet using the 'Weeder Tool,' making sure only the design remains on the clear liner.

Using the 'Cricut Easy Press Mini' and 'Easy Press Mat,' the iron-on layers can be easily transferred to your mug.

Preheat your 'Easy Press Mini,' put your design on the desired area, and apply pressure for a couple of minutes or more. Wait for few minutes before peeling off the design while it is still warm.

CUSTOMIZED DOORMAT

MATERIALS NEEDED:

-Cricut Machine
-Scrap cardstock (The color does not matter)
-Coir mat (18" x 30')
-Outdoor acrylic paint

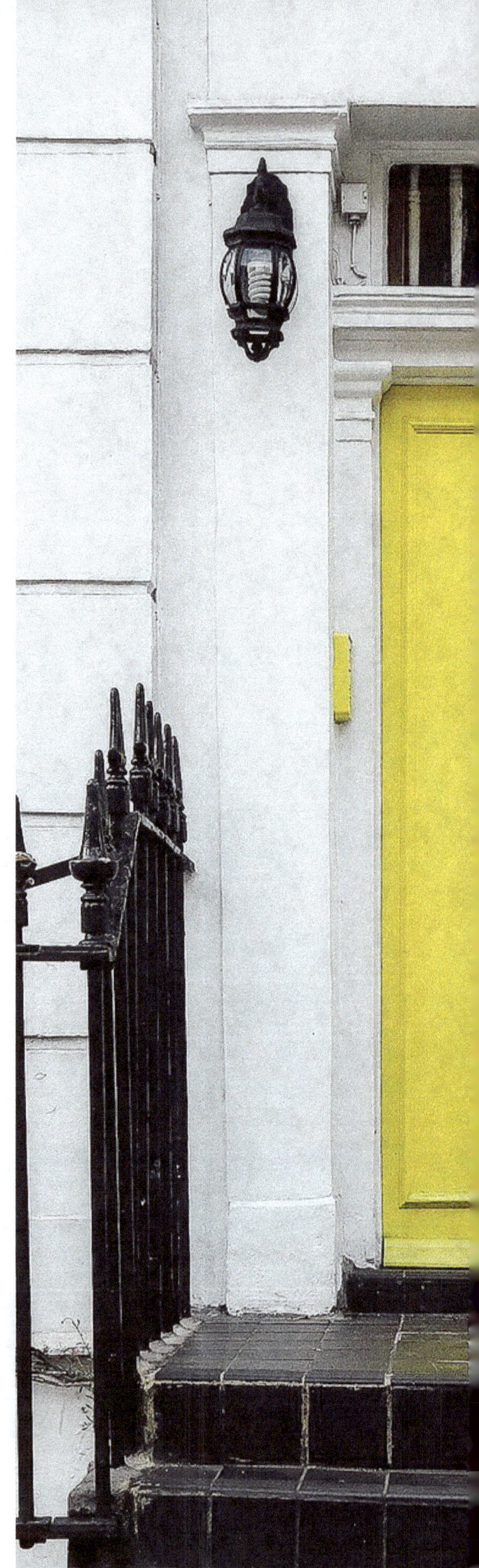

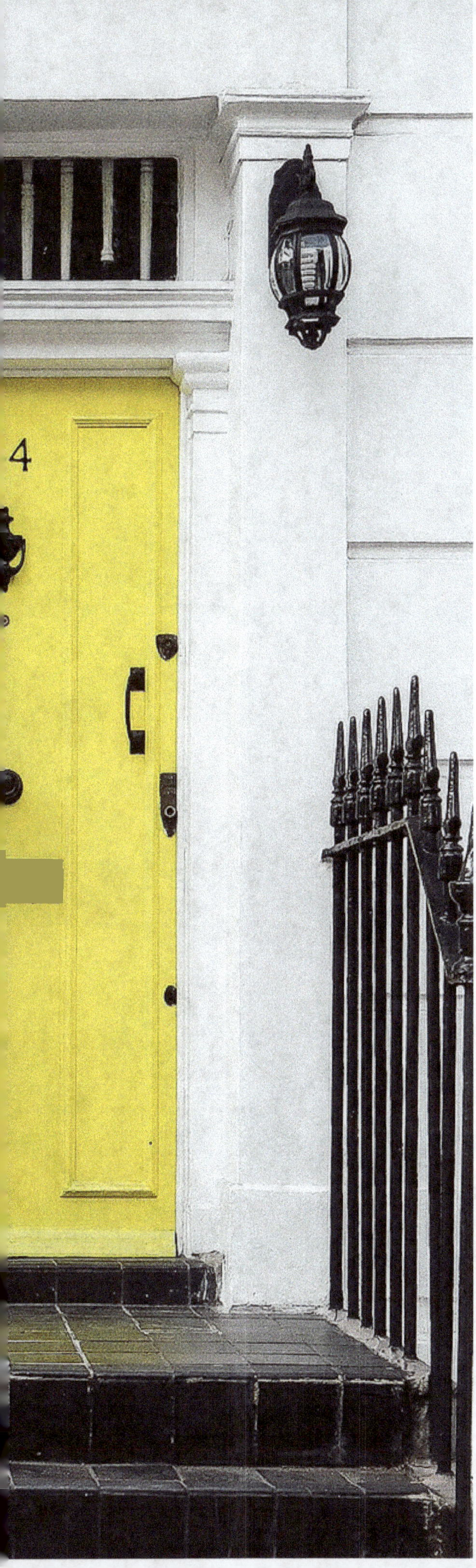

-Vinyl stencil
-Transfer tape
-Flat round paintbrush
-Cutting mat (12" x 24")

DIRECTIONS

Create your design in Cricut Design Space. You can also download an SVG design of your choice and import it into Cricut Design Space. Make sure that your design is the right size; resize it to ensure that this is so.

Next, you are to cut the stencil. You do this by clicking "Make it" in Cricut Design Space when done with the design. After this, you select "Cardstock" as the material. Then, you press the "Cut" button on the Cricut machine. When this is done, remove the stencil from the machine and weed.

Next, on the reverse side of the stencil, apply spray glue. After this, attach the stencil to the doormat, exactly where you want your design to be; then, pick up the letter bits left on the cutting mat and glue them to their places in the stencil on the doormat.

The next step is to mask the doormat's parts that you do not want to paint on. You can do this using painters' plastic.

Now, it's time to spray-paint your stencil on the doormat. Keeping the paint can about 5 inches away from the doormat, spray up and down, keeping the can point straight through the stencil. If it is at an angle, the paint will get under the stencil and ruin your design. Spray the entire stencil 2-3 times to ensure that you do not miss any part and that the paint is even.

You're just about done! Now, remove the masking plastic and the stencil and leave the doormat for about one hour to get dry.

GLITTER TUMBLER

MATERIALS NEEDED

-Painters tape
-Mod podge and paintbrush
-Epoxy
-Glitter
-Stainless steel tumbler
-Spray paint
-Vinyl
-Sandpaper Wet/dry
-Gloves
-Plastic cup
-Measuring cup
-Rubbing alcohol

DIRECTIONS

Now that we have got your materials, so let us look at the Direction to making this work:
Tape off the top and bottom of the tumbler.
Make sure to seal them well enough that paint will not get on either side.
Spray paint twelve inches away from your tumbler in an area that is well ventilated.
Make sure that the items you used are approved and will not make you sick.

Once your tumbler is dry from the paint you have used, you can add the glitter.

This will make a mess, so have something under it to catch the glitter.

Put the mod podge in a small container.

Use a flat paintbrush to put it on.

Take the lid off, and rotate the cup adding glitter gradually.

Make sure it is completely covered.

Make sure that an excess glitter will come off before removing the tape and letting it dry.

When dry, take a clean flat brush and stroke down the glitter to get any additional pieces not glued down.

Add a piece of tape above the glitter line.

Do the same to the bottom.

Get a plastic cup and gloves.

Use the epoxy, and measure equal parts of solution A and B into measuring cups. If it is a small mug, you only need about 15 ml each. Larger ones need 20 ml.

Pour them both in a cup, and scrape down the sides using a wooden stick.

Stir for three minutes and pop all bubbles.

Your gloves should be on, but if not, put them on now.

Add the glitter to the epoxy and stir.

Add the mixture to the tumbler, and turn it often while you are doing this. Having a roller or something to turn it on will help make sure it is in the air, so nothing is touching it.

When the drugs are not coming as fast, slow the turning down and make sure the turning is constant.

Take the tape off after forty-five minutes.

Spin the tumbler for five hours; it should be dry; if

not, leave it on a foam roller overnight.

Sand the tumbler gently with wet sandpaper.

When it is all smooth from sanding, clean it with rubbing alcohol.

Then open the Cricut design space, and cut out your glitter vinyl.

Weed the design.

Add a strong grip transfer tape.

Transfer the decal to the tumbler.

This is a challenging project that takes a lot of time, and you need to make sure that children are nowhere near these products as it will be fatal to them if they swallow them. Another thing to remember is spinning and making sure it is dry. By following these instructions, you should have a perfect glitter tumbler that you can take anywhere and rock a stylish look. This is an excellent idea for business owners because decorated tumblers are a hot commodity right now, and everyone loves them.

VINYL CHALKBOARD

MATERIALS NEEDED:

-Cricut Maker or Cricut Explore
-Standard Grip mat
-Cricut Linen vinyl in desired colors
-Weeder, transfer tape
-Chalkboard and chalk pen

DIRECTION

Log into the 'Design Space' application and click

on the 'New Project' button on the screen's top right corner to view a blank canvas.

Click on the 'Projects' icon and type in 'Vinyl Chalkboard' in the search bar.

Click on 'Customize' to edit the project to your preference further, click on the 'Make It's a button, load the vinyl sheet to your Cricut machine, and follow the Direction the screen to cut your project.

Using a Weeder tool, remove the negative space pieces of the design.

Use the transfer tape to apply the vinyl cuts to the chalkboard. Then use the scraper tool on top of the transfer tape to remove any bubbles, and then just peel off the transfer tape.

Lastly, use a chalk pen to write messages.

VINYL HERRINGBONE BRACELET

MATERIALS NEEDED:

-Cricut Maker or Cricut Explore
-Standard Grip mat
-Vinyl (midnight)
-Weeder
-Scraper
-Transfer tape
-Metal bracelet gold

DIRECTION

Log into the 'Design Space' application and click on the 'New Project' button on the screen's

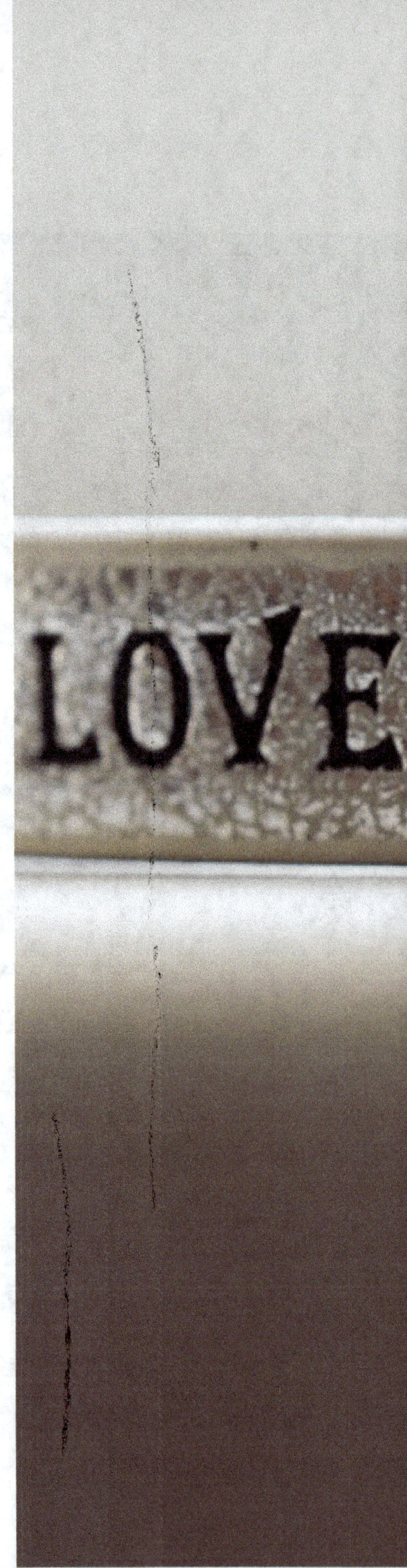

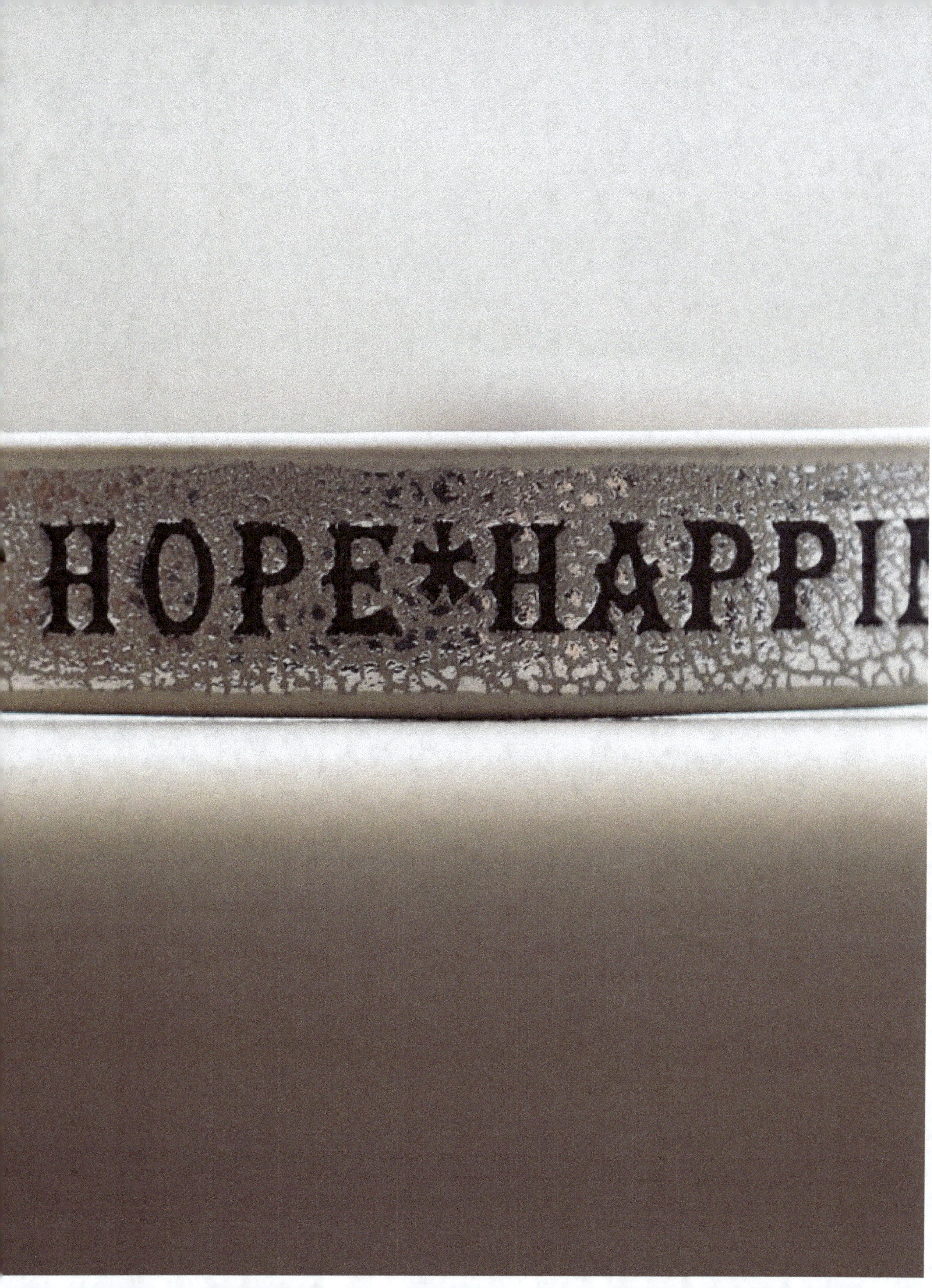

HOPE*HAPPIN

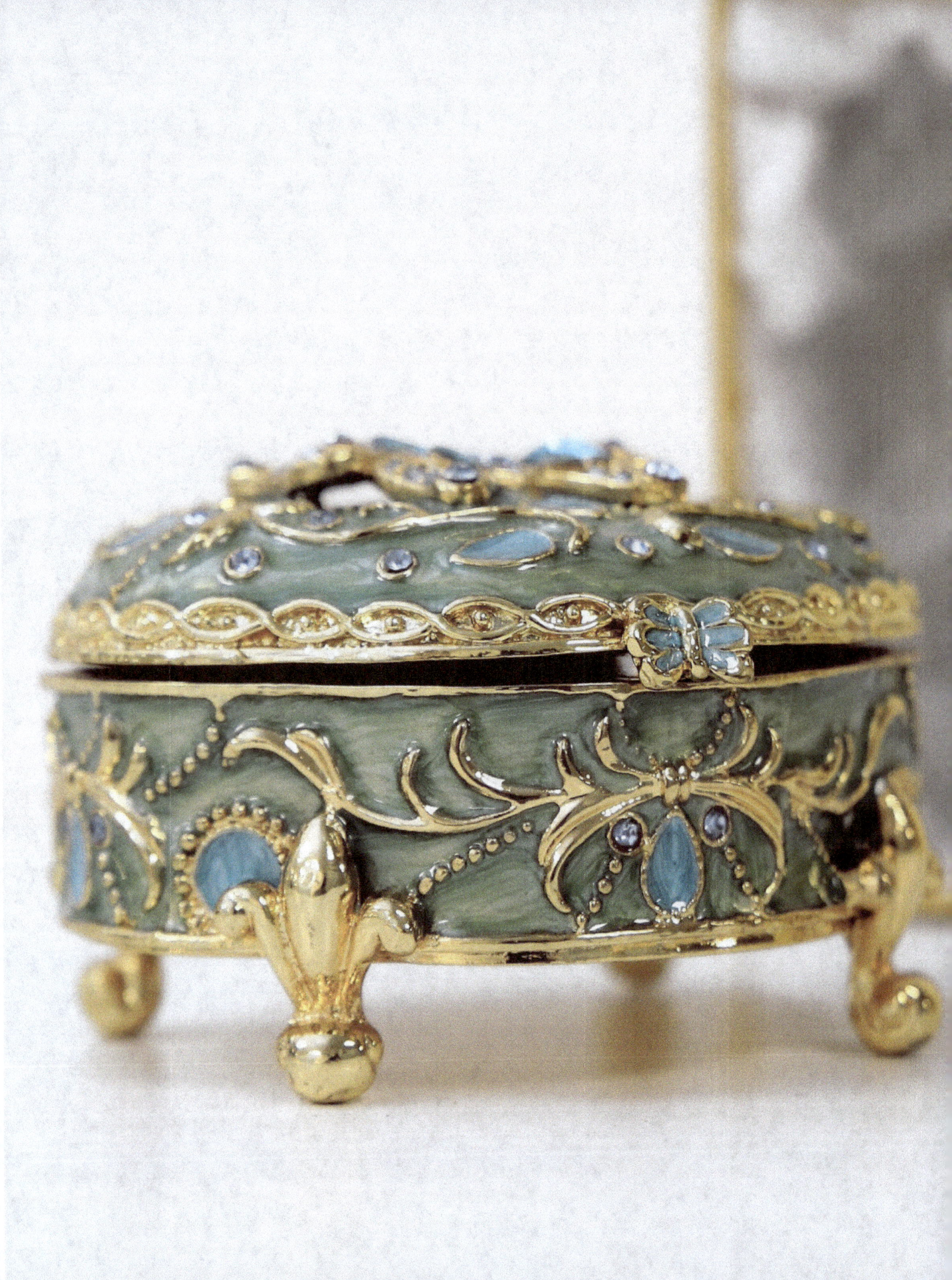

top right corner to view a blank canvas.

Click on the 'Images' icon on the 'Design Panel,' and type in '#M33278' in the search bar. Select the image and click on the 'Insert Images' button at the bottom of the screen.

Click on 'Customize' to edit the project to your preference further, or simply click on the 'Make It' button, load the vinyl sheet to your Cricut machine, and follow the Directionon the screen cut your project.

Using a Weeder tool, remove the negative space pieces of the design. Use the transfer tape to apply the vinyl cuts to the bracelet. Then use the scraper tool on top of the transfer tape to remove any bubbles, and then just peel off the transfer tape.

TREASURE CHEST JEWELRY BOX

MATERIALS NEEDED

-Plain wooden box with lid
-White vinyl
-Vinyl transfer tape
-Cutting mat
-Weeding tool or pick   Small blade

DIRECTION

Select the "Image" button in the lower left-hand corner and search for "keyhole."
Click your favorite keyhole design and click "Insert."
Select the "Text" button in the lower left-hand corner.
Choose your favorite font and type "Treasure."
Place your vinyl on the cutting mat.

Send design to Cricut.

Make use of a weeding tool or pick to remove the excess vinyl from the design.

Apply separate pieces of transfer tape to the keyhole and the word.

Remove the paper backing from the tape on the keyhole.

Place the keyhole where the lid and box meet so that half is on the lid and half is on the box.

Rub the tape to transfer the vinyl to the wood, making sure there are no bubbles. Carefully peel the tape away.

Use a sharp blade to cut the keyhole design in half so that the box can open.

Transfer the word to the front of the box using the same method.

Optional: Add details with paint or markers to make the box look more like a treasure chest. Add wood grain, barnacles, seashells, or pearls.

Store your jewelry in your new treasure chest!

MOTIVATIONAL WATER BOTTLE

MATERIALS NEEDED

-Sturdy water bottle of your choice
-Glitter vinyl
-Vinyl transfer tape
-Light grip cutting mat
-Weeding tool or pick

DIRECTION

Measure the space on your water bottle where you

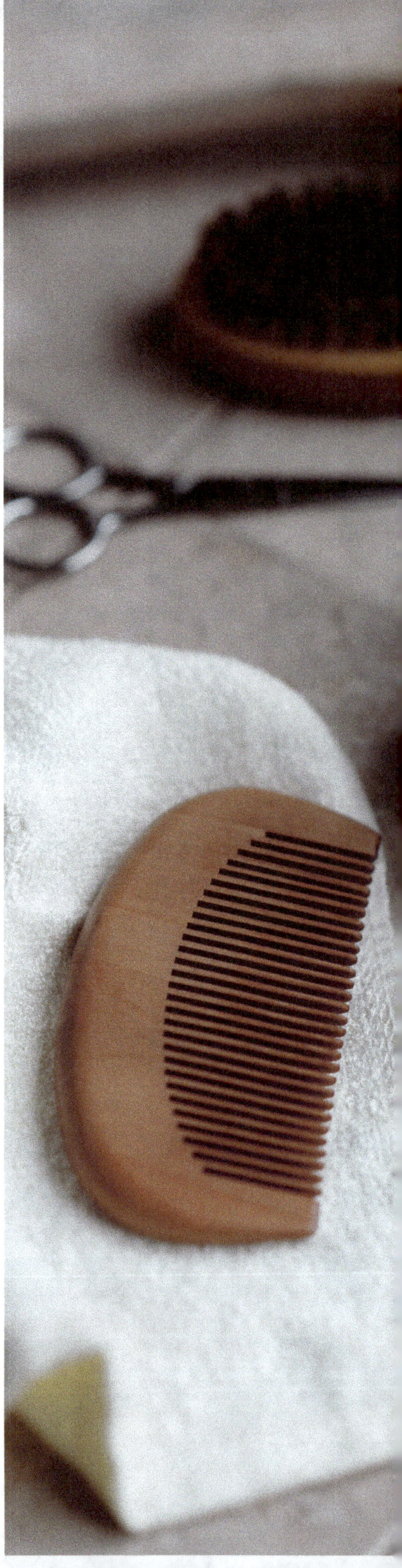

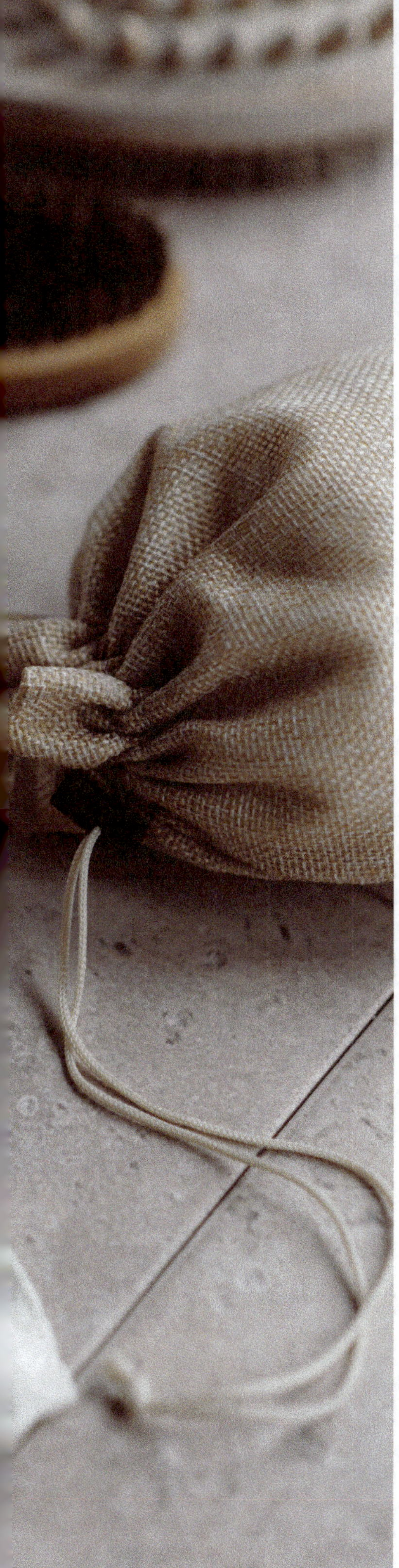

want the text and create a box that size.

Select the "Text" button in the lower left-hand corner.

Choose your favorite font and type the motivational quote you like best.

I sweat glitter

Sweat is magic

I don't sweat; I sparkle

Place the vinyl on the cutting mat.

Send the design to Cricut.

Use a weeding tool or pick to remove the excess vinyl from the text.

Apply transfer tape to the quote.

Remove the paper backing from the tape.

Place the quote where you want it on the water bottle.

Rub the tape to transfer the vinyl to the bottle, making sure there are no bubbles. Carefully peel the tape away.

Bring your new water bottle to the gym for motivation and hydration!

CUSTOMIZED MAKEUP BAG

MATERIALS NEEDED

-Pink fabric makeup bag

-Purple heat transfer vinyl

-Cricut EasyPress or iron

-Cutting mat

-Weeding tool or pick

-Keychain or charm of your choice

DIRECTION

Measure the space on your makeup bag where you want the design and create a box that size.
Select the "Image" button in the lower left-hand corner and search "monogram."
Choose your favorite monogram and click "Insert."
Place vinyl on the cutting mat.
Send the design to your Cricut.
Use a weeding tool or pick to remove the excess vinyl from the design.
Place the design on the bag with the plastic side up.
Carefully iron on the design.
After cooling, peel away the plastic by rolling it.
Hang your charm or keychain off the zipper.
Stash your makeup in your customized bag!

PERPETUAL CALENDAR

MATERIALS NEEDED

-Unfinished woodblock calendar
-Acrylic paint in the color(s) of your choosing.
-Vinyl color(s) of your choosing
-Vinyl transfer tape
-Cutting mat
-Weeding tool or pick
-Mod Podge

DIRECTION

Paint the woodblock calendar in the colors you'd like and set it aside to dry.
Open Cricut Design Space and create a new project.

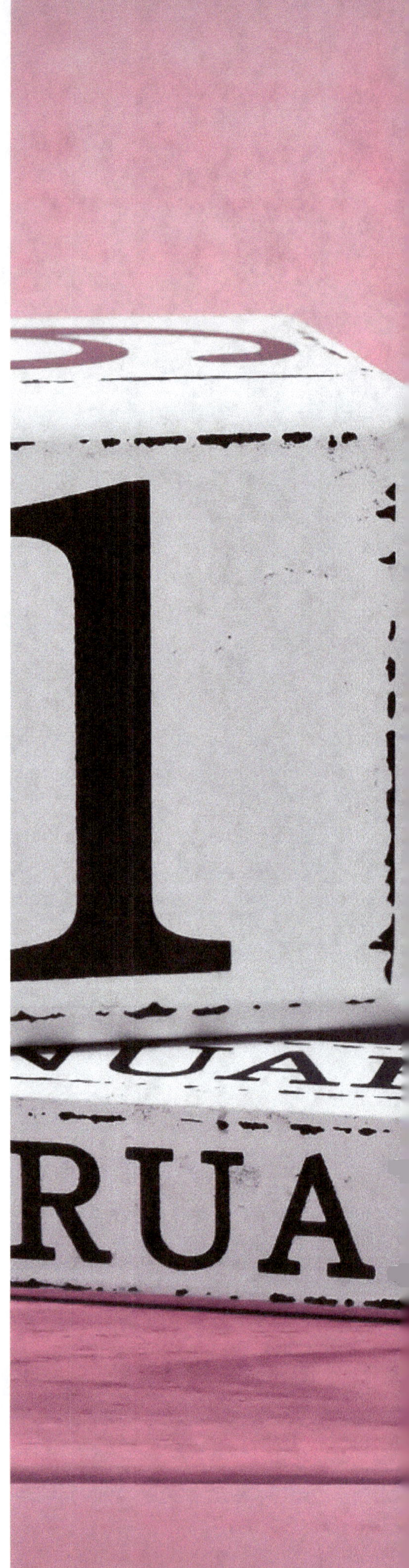

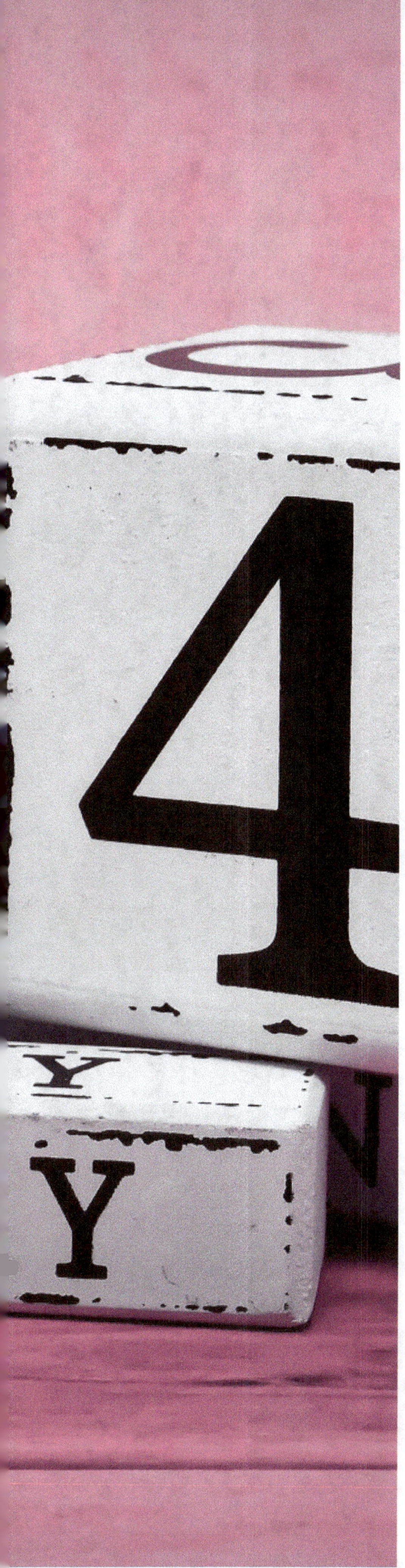

Create a square of the correct size for the four blocks.

Select the "Text" button.

Choose your favorite font, and type the following numbers as well as all of the months: 0, 0, 1, 1, 2, 2, 3, 4, 5, 6, 7, 8

Place your vinyl on the mat.

Send design to your Cricut.

Make use of a weeding tool or pick to remove the excess vinyl from the text.

Apply transfer tape to each separate number and the months.

Remove the paper backing from the tape and apply for the numbers as follows.

0 and 5 on the top and bottom of the first block

1, 2, 3, 4 around the sides of the first block

0 and 8 on the top and bottom of the second block

1, 2, 6, 7 around the sides of the second block

Remove the paper backing from the tape on the months, and apply them to the long blocks, the first six months on one and the second six months on the other.

Rub the tape to transfer the vinyl to the wood, making sure there are no bubbles.

Carefully peel the tape away.

Seal everything with a coat of Mod Podge.

Arrange your calendar to display today's date and enjoy it year after year!

Chapter 4
Iron on and Heat Transfer Vinyl HTV crafts

PERSONALIZED MUGS (IRON-ON VINYL)

MATERIALS NEEDED:

-Cricut Maker or Cricut Explore
-Standard Grip mat
-Printable Cricut iron-on or heat transfer vinyl
-Cricut Easy Press Mini
-Easy Press mat
-Weeding tool
-Ceramic mug

DIRECTION

Log into the 'Design Space' application and click on the 'New Project' button on the screen's top right corner to view a blank canvas.

Click on the 'Images' icon on the 'Design Panel' and type in 'America' in the search bar. Click on the desired image, then click on the 'Insert Images' button at the screen's bottom.

Click on the 'Templates' icon on the 'Designs Panel' located on the left of the screen, type in 'Mug' in the templates search bar, and select the mug icon.

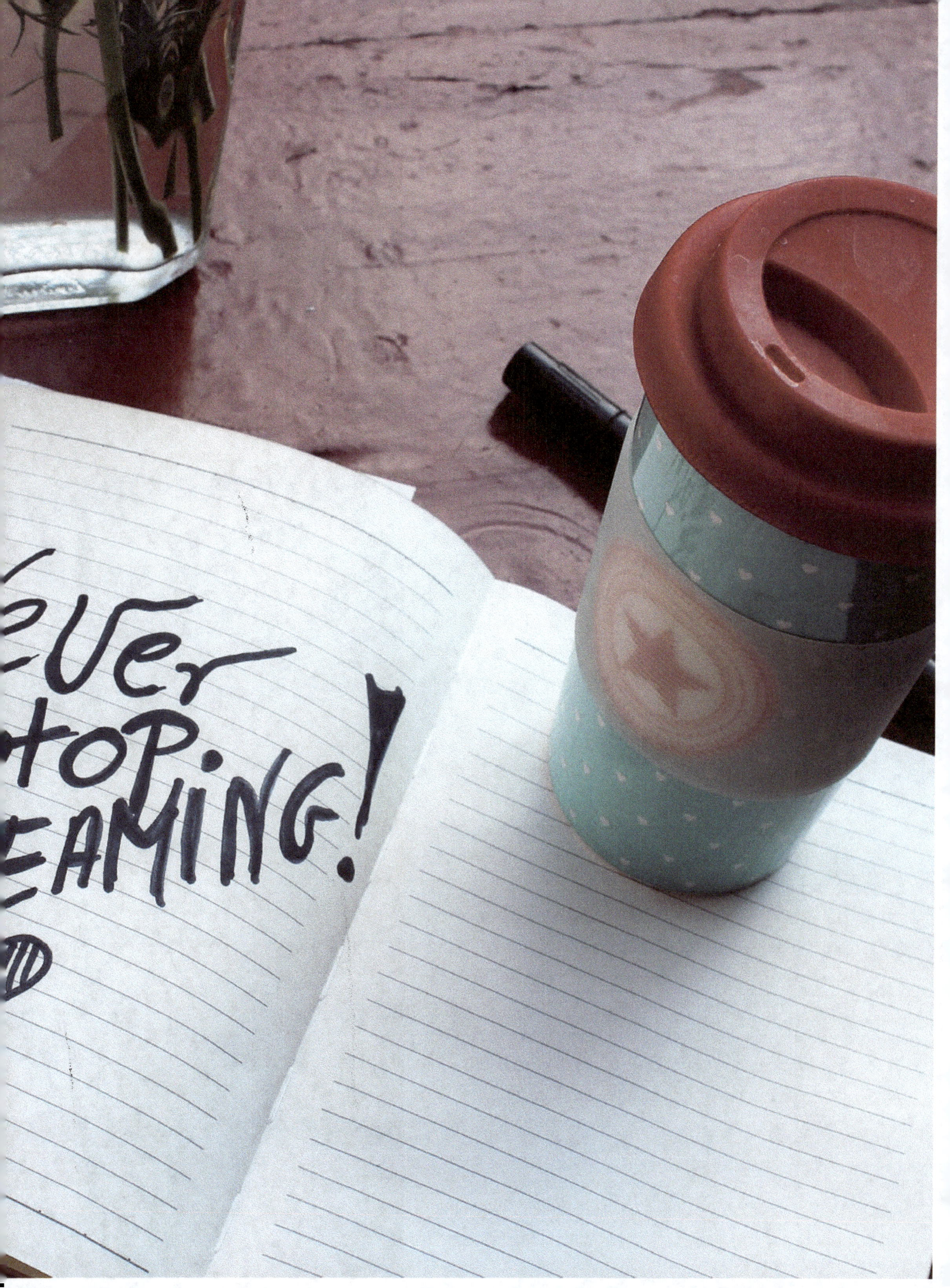
EVER
STOP
DREAMING!

You can change the 'Type' and 'Size' of the template to decorate mugs with non-standard sizes by clicking on the 'Size' icon and selecting 'Custom' to update your mug size.

You can further edit your design by clicking on the 'Shapes' icon adding: hearts, stars, or other desired shapes to your design.

Click on 'Save' at the top right corner of the screen and give the desired name to the project, for example, 'Mug Decoration' and click 'Save.'

The design is ready to be printed and cut. Simply click on the 'Make It' button, and follow the prompts on the screen for using the inkjet printer to print the design on your printable iron-on vinyl, and subsequently, cut the design.

Note: One side of the Printable Iron-on Dark sheet is white with a matte finish; the other side is printed with blue grid lines. Print on the flat side; the side with the blue gridlines is the iron-on backing removed before applying your design to your material.

Carefully remove the excess material from the sheet using the 'Weeder Tool,' making sure only the design remains on the clear liner.

Using the 'Cricut Easy Press Mini' and 'Easy Press Mat,' the iron-on layers can be easily transferred to your mug. Preheat your 'Easy Press Mini' and put your design on the desired area and apply pressure for a couple of minutes or more (Sample project in the picture below). Wait for few minutes before peeling off the design while it is still warm. (Since the design is delicate, use the spatula tool or your fingers to rub the letters down the mug before starting to peel the design).

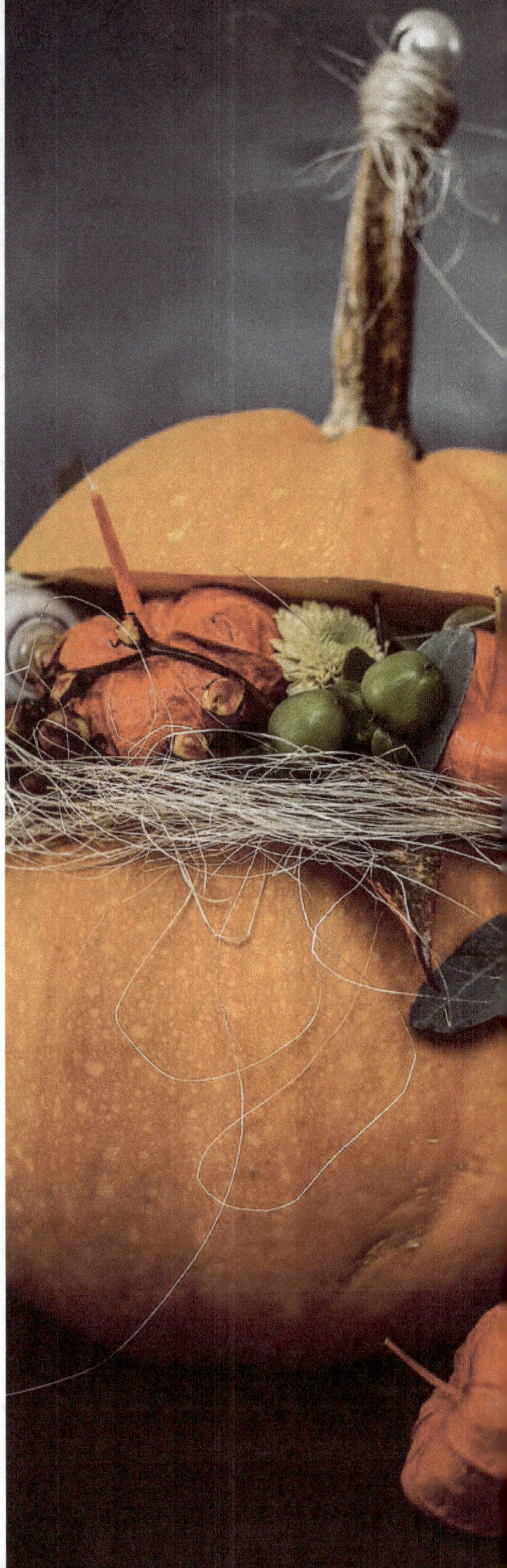

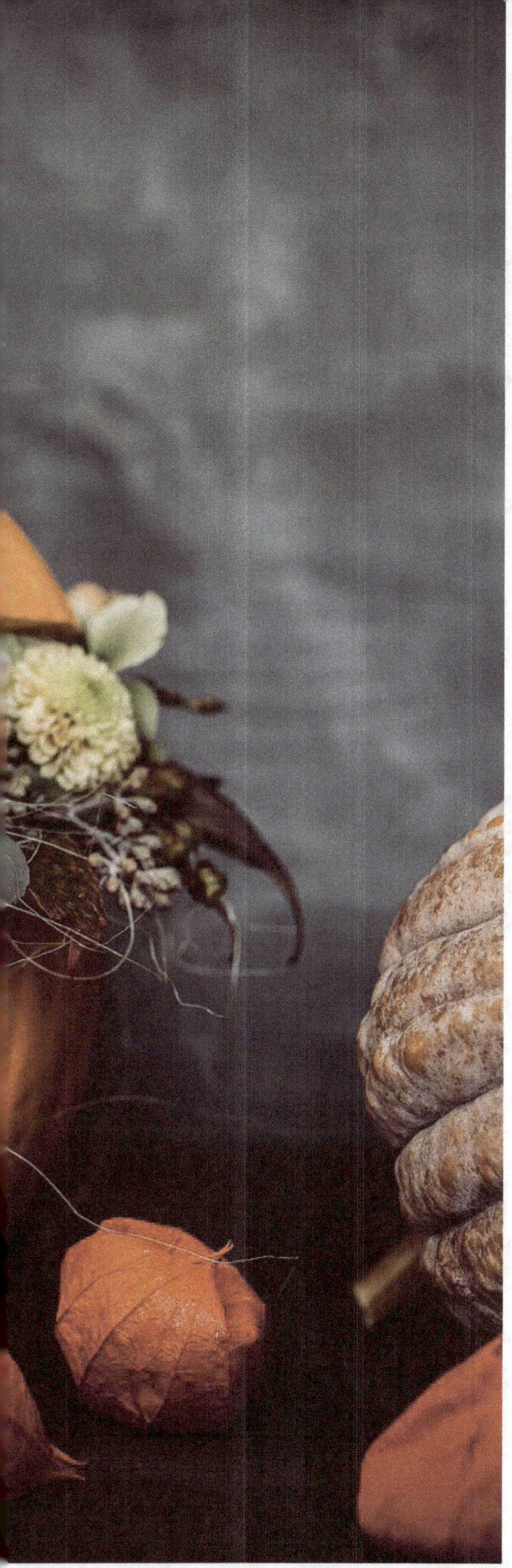

HALLOWEEN PUMPKIN VINYL DESIGN

MATERIALS NEEDED

-Vinyl in your preference of paint
-Transfer Tape
-Cricut Machine
-Simple Pumpkins
-SVG file

DIRECTIONS

Gathering materials. You will need a plain pumpkin, art vinyl (you can pick whatever vinyl and shades you prefer), a Rae Dunn template and use the Vector format document, a Cricut machine, and a tape transfer (you can need this to apply the tapered text to the pumpkins).

Scale the picture according to the pumpkin's size. The picture should be about 4 x 6 inches in dimension.

Break the image and weed it (delete the undesirable aspect of the slashed image, eliminate the outside around the letters in this case).

When you add to the pumpkin, attach transfer tape to your cut picture to scale and scrape away the transfer tape.

FATHER'S DAY MUG

MATERIALS NEEDED

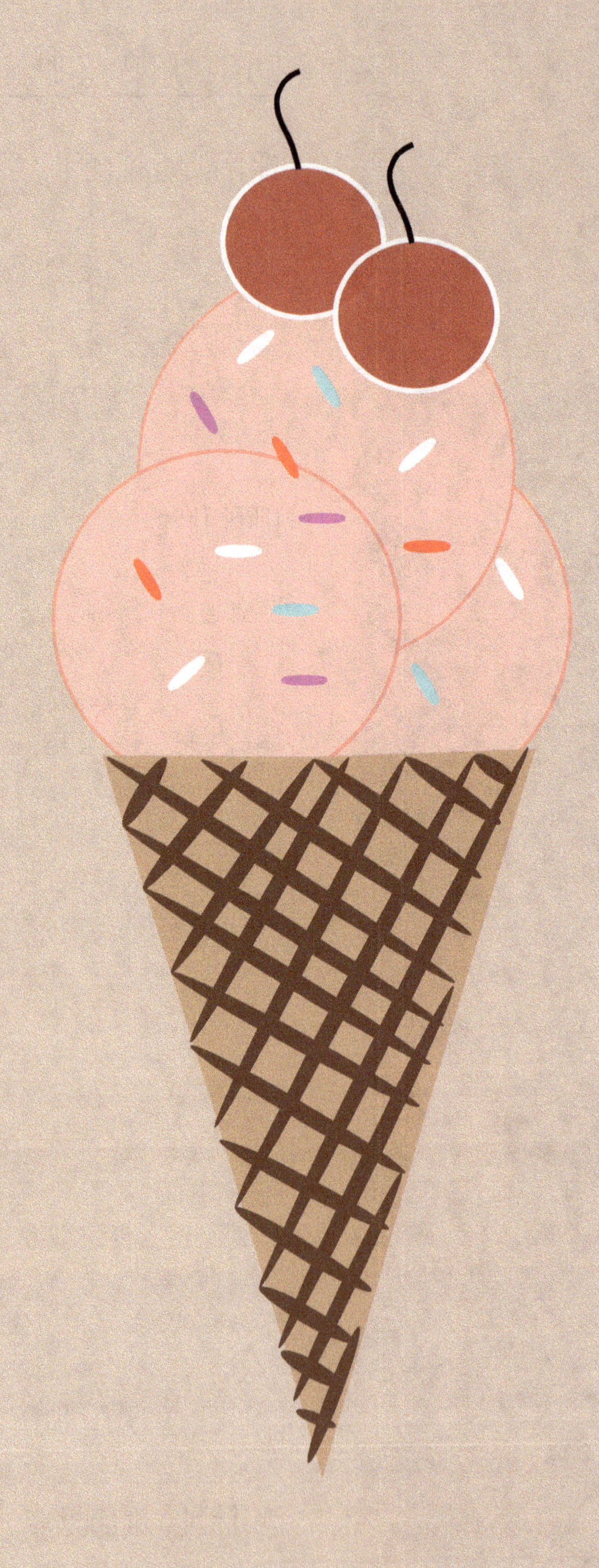

-Stuff
-Cricut computer and Cricut-design room
-SVG cut file produced by Jen Goode for Father's -Day
-Vinyl Blue
-A cup or mug

DIRECTIONS:

Download and upload the file that was cut from the SVG to the Cricut Machine Space.

Set the file to the size you'd want and look at it. I sized my mug to around 3.5" high. The on-screen directions for cutting the term art add.

The leftover vinyl that falls from your building needs to be weeded.

Using the transfer tape, place the term art on the dry and clean side of the cup. To fit in, burnish.

It is that! Super-fast and straightforward, huh?

Humor from Cut Dad Jen Goode's designed word painting. Then, the transfer tape is

Used with vinyl word art to modify the cup. Build a gift for your dad, Cricut. Word art is an excellent source of DIY crafts for every type of style.

ICE CREAM CONES COVERS

MATERIALS NEEDED

-Large-sized needle
-Text-weight or card inventory certificates
-Low-temp hot glue handgun
-Double-sided roller adhesive
-The Twine of the Pink Baker
-Vinyl iron-on

-Iron-on vinyl cutting uni
-Scissors
-Weeding method
-Surface iron and ironing
-Smooth cotton fabric for ironing

DIRECTIONS:

Break a text-weight or board stock document flag. To protect strong backs on cut banner fronts, use double-sided adhesive.

Via cracks, connect parts with a wide needle by adding the pink baker's twine.

Sliced from letter-weight or card stock paper for cone wraps. Form the paper on the edge of the table softly, then cover it with hot glue.

Break the iron-on vinyl parts with the mat facing the polished plastic side and mirror the split. From templates, peel waste.

Using the weeding method to delete all the information from the parts.

On the front of the apron put the text piece and the cone piece.

Hot iron, no steam, then iron in place.

Remove the plastic from the pattern softly at a tight angle.

One by one, there are iron surfaces of ice cream and strawberry, beginning from the bottom and going up.

Tip: note to use a smooth fabric ironing cloth to cover the final design and give it a final push with the hot iron to seal the design. Do not strike the iron on the exposed iron-on vinyl directly since it can burn

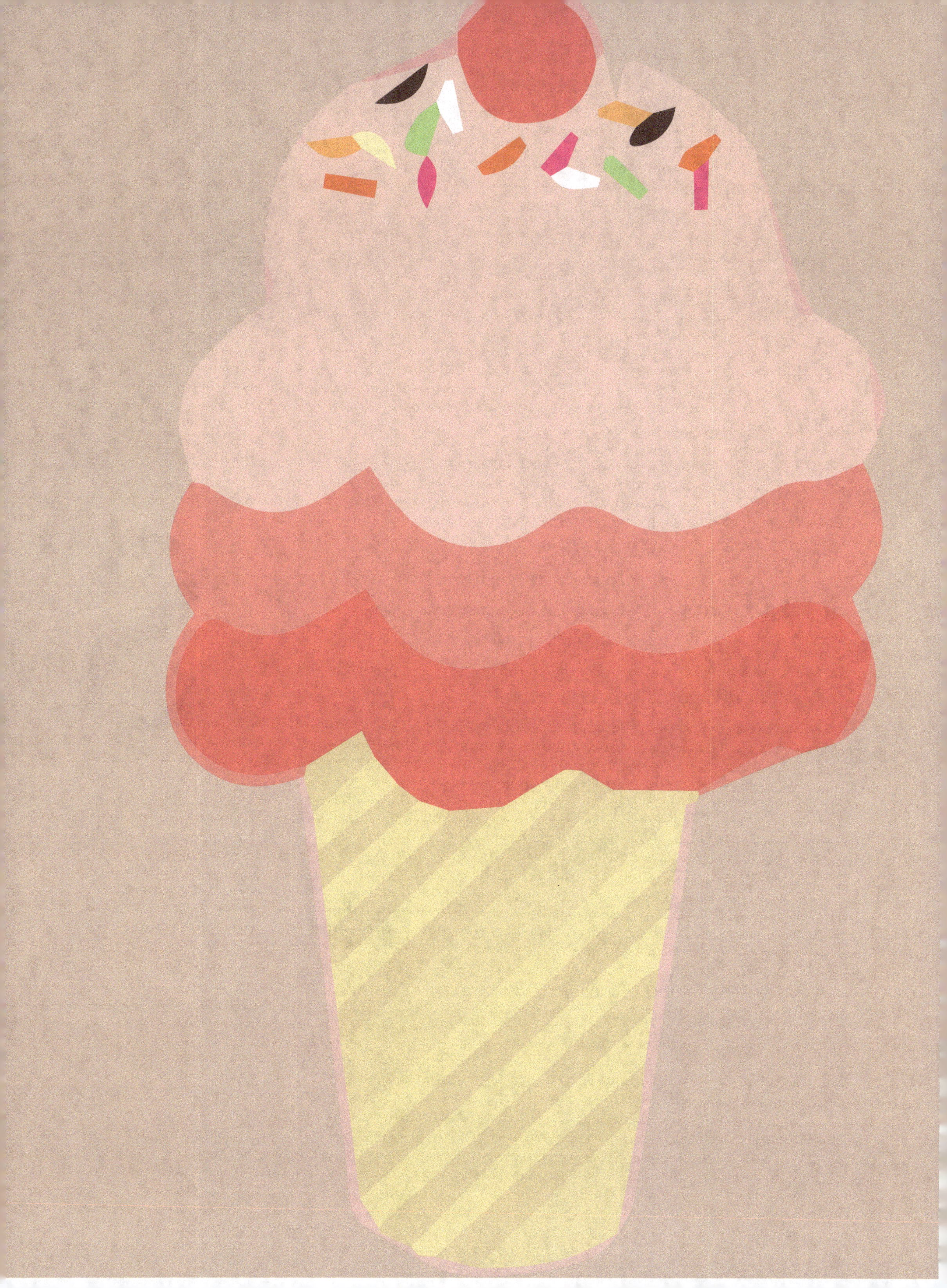

CUSTOM GRAPHIC T—SHIRT?

MATERIALS NEEDED

-The Cricut machine
-Vinyl for the letters
-Your Cricut tools kit

DIRECTION

Start by choosing the image you want to use. This can be done in Photoshop, or you can place your text directly into the Design Space.

Next, open the Cricut Design Space. Choose the canvas you wish to use by clicking the 'Canvas' icon on the dashboard, located on the left-hand side. Select the canvas that you will be using for your vinyl letters. This can be anything within the categories they offer.

Then, select the size of the shirt for the canvas. This is located on the right-hand side of the options.

Now, click 'Upload' for uploading your image, which is located on the left-hand side. Select the image you are using by browsing the list of ideas in your file library. Then, select the type of image that you have picked. For most projects, especially iron-on ones, you will choose the Simple Cut option.

Click on the white space that you want to be removed by cutting out. Remember to cut the insides of every letter.

Next, be super diligent and press 'Cut Image' instead of 'Print First.' You do not want to print the image simply; you cut it as well.

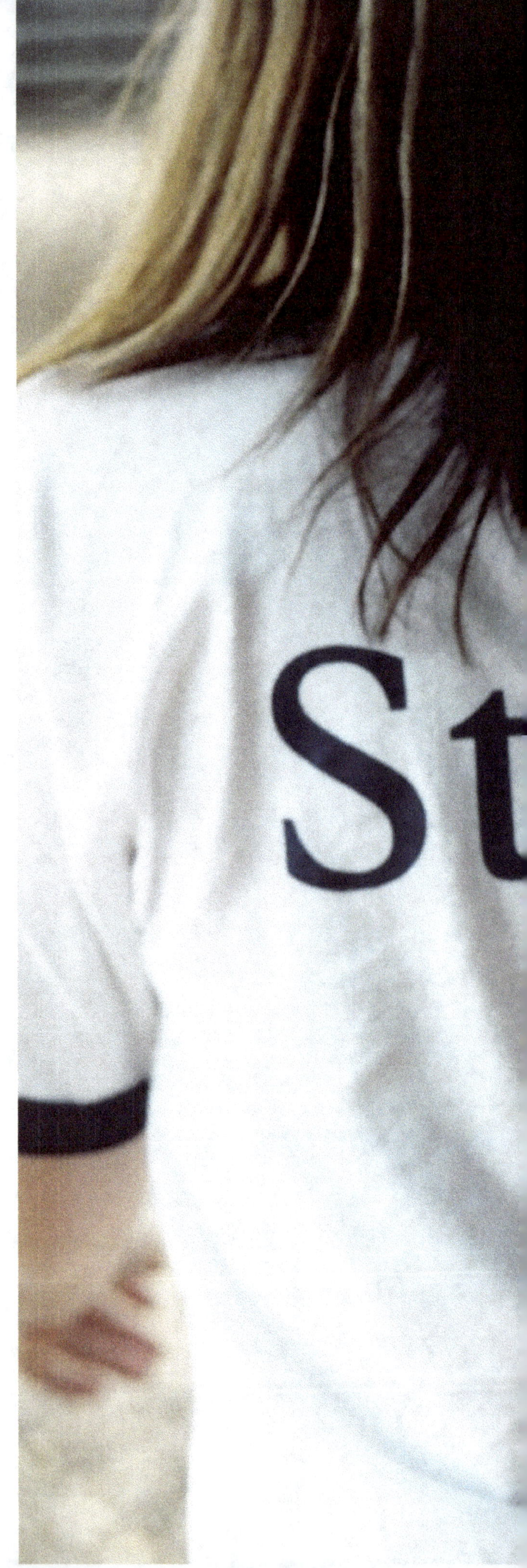

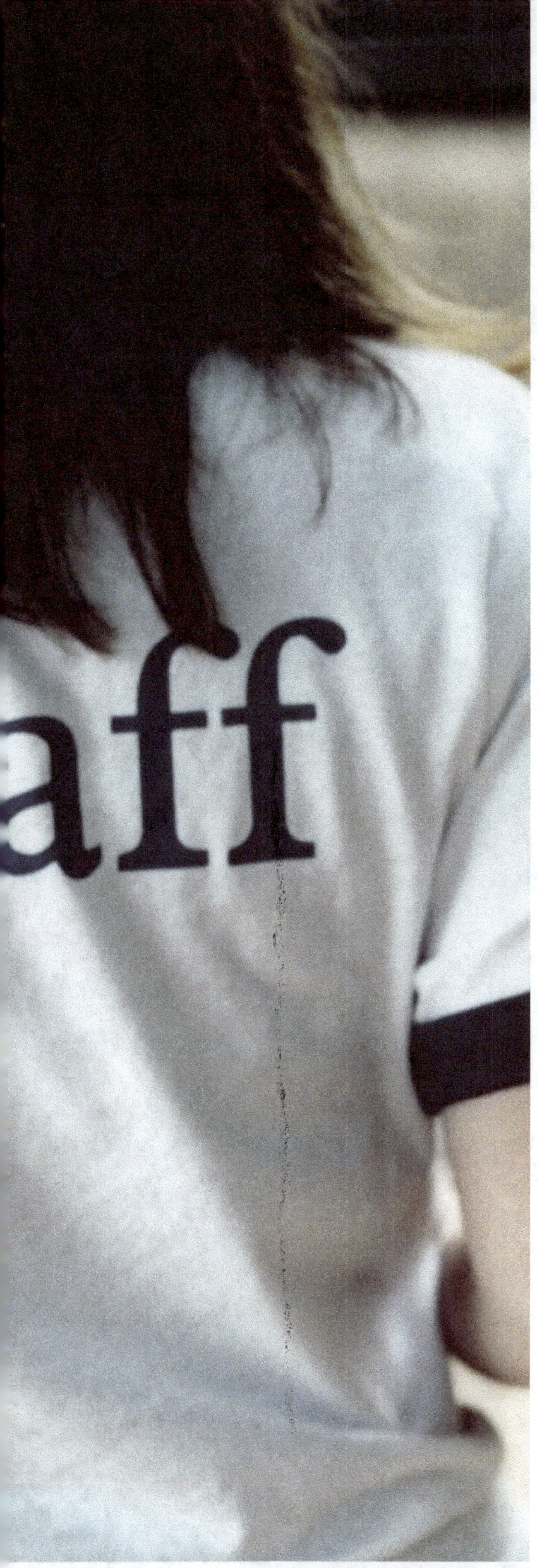

Place the image on your chosen canvas and adjust the sizing of the picture.

Place your iron-on image with the vinyl side facing down on the mat, and then turn the dial to the setting for 'Iron-On.'

Next, you will want to click the 'Mirror Image' setting for the image before hitting 'Go.'

Once you have cut the image, you should remove the excess vinyl from the edges around the lettering or image. Then use the tool for weeding out the inner pieces of the letters.

Now you will be placing the vinyl on the shirt. And now, the fun part begins. You will get to iron the image onto the shirt. Using the cotton setting, you will need to use the hottest setting to get your iron too. There should not be any steam.

You want to warm the shirt by placing the iron on the shirt portion to hold the image. This should be warmed up for 15 seconds.

Next, lay the vinyl out exactly where you want it to be placed. Place a pressing cloth over the top of the plastic.

This will prevent the plastic on the shirt from melting.

Place your iron onto the pressing cloth for around 30 seconds. Flip the shirt and place the pressing cloth and iron on the backside of the vinyl.

Flip your shirt back over, and begin to peel off the sticky part of the vinyl that you have been overlaying on the shirt. This will separate the vinyl from the plastic backing. This should be done while the plastic and vinyl are hot.

If you are having trouble removing the vinyl from the plastic backing, then place the iron back on the part that is being difficult. Then proceed to pull up, and it should come off nicely.

This should remove the plastic from the vinyl that is now on the shirt. Place the pressing cloth on top of the vinyl once again, and heat it to ensure that it is good and stuck.

CUSTOMIZED SOCK

MATERIALS NEEDED

-Cricut Maker or Cricut Explore,
-standard grip mat,
-Everyday iron-on (recommended 'Sportflex Iron-On' or heat-transfer vinyl, socks,
-Cricut EasyPress, EasyPress mat,
-weeding tool

DIRECTION

After you have logged into your Cricut account on Design Space, click on the New Project button on the top-right corner of the screen to start a new project. A blank canvas will be displayed.

Let us use text for this project. Click on Text from the Design panel on the left of the screen, and type in "IF YOU CAN READ THIS" and "BRING ME PIZZA" or any other phrases you may like. We want the text to be horizontal for the sock, so just press Enter after each word to move it down to the next line. Click on Alignment, then Center, to align the text as shown in the picture below.

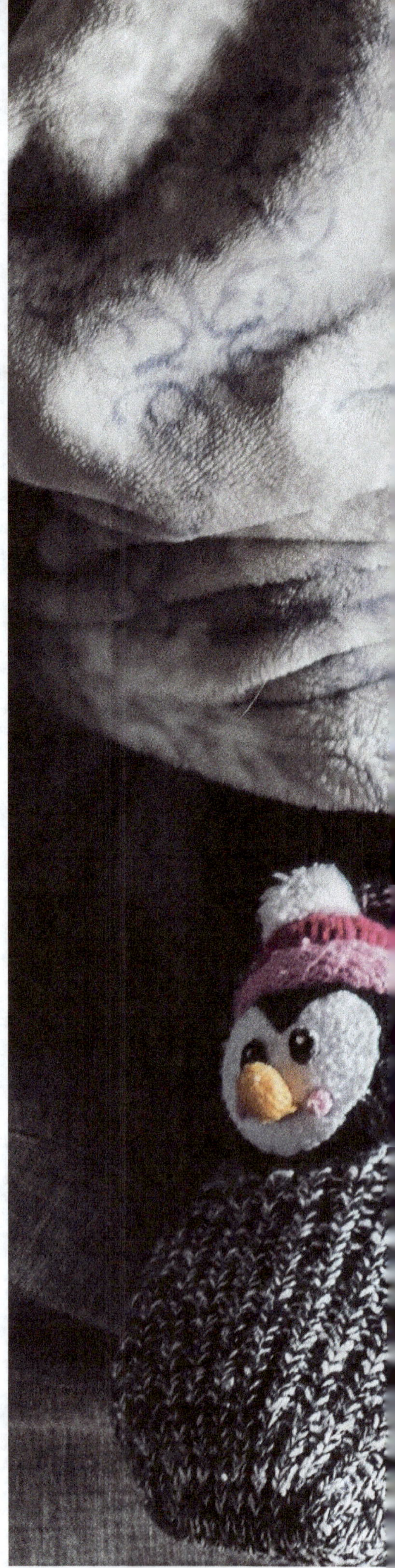

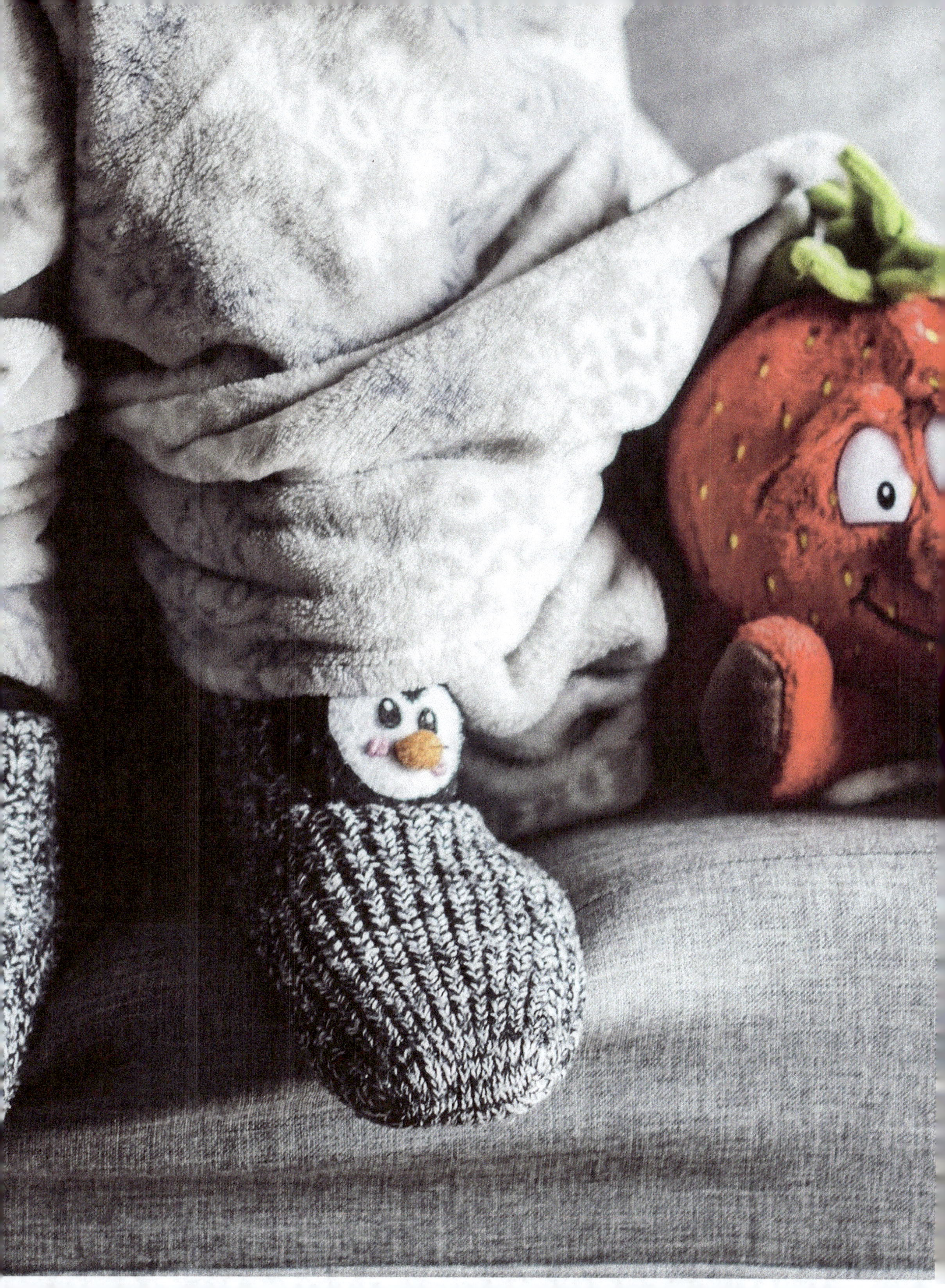

For the image below, the font Alleycat ICG in Regular, the color shown in the picture below were selected. But you can let your creativity take over this step and choose any color or font you like. Select and copy-paste your image the number of times you want to print your design.

Click on Save at the top-right corner of the screen, and give the desired name to the project, for example, 'Sock Project.' Click Save.

Simply click on the Make It button on the top-right corner of the screen. You will see the required mats and material displayed on the screen. Make sure you click on the Mirror button under the Material Size on the left of the screen.

Load the iron-on in your desired color to your Cricut machine, and click Continue at the bottom-right corner of the screen to start cutting your design.

Once your Cricut device has been connected to your computer, set your cut setting to Iron-On. Place the iron-on with its shiny side (clear liner down, on the cutting mat). Load your mat into your Cricut machine. Design Space will guide you through the cutting of the image. Carefully remove the excess material from the sheet using the weeder tool, ensuring only the design remains on the clear liner. Using the Cricut EasyPress and EasyPress Mat, the iron-on layers can be easily transferred to your sock. The recommended temperature for Sportflex Iron-On material and cotton base material is 05 °F. So, preheat your EasyPress.

Put your design on the desired area and apply pressure for 0 seconds. Then flip your sock to apply the heat and pressure for another 5 seconds on the other side. Wait for a couple of minutes before peeling off the design while it is still warm. (Since

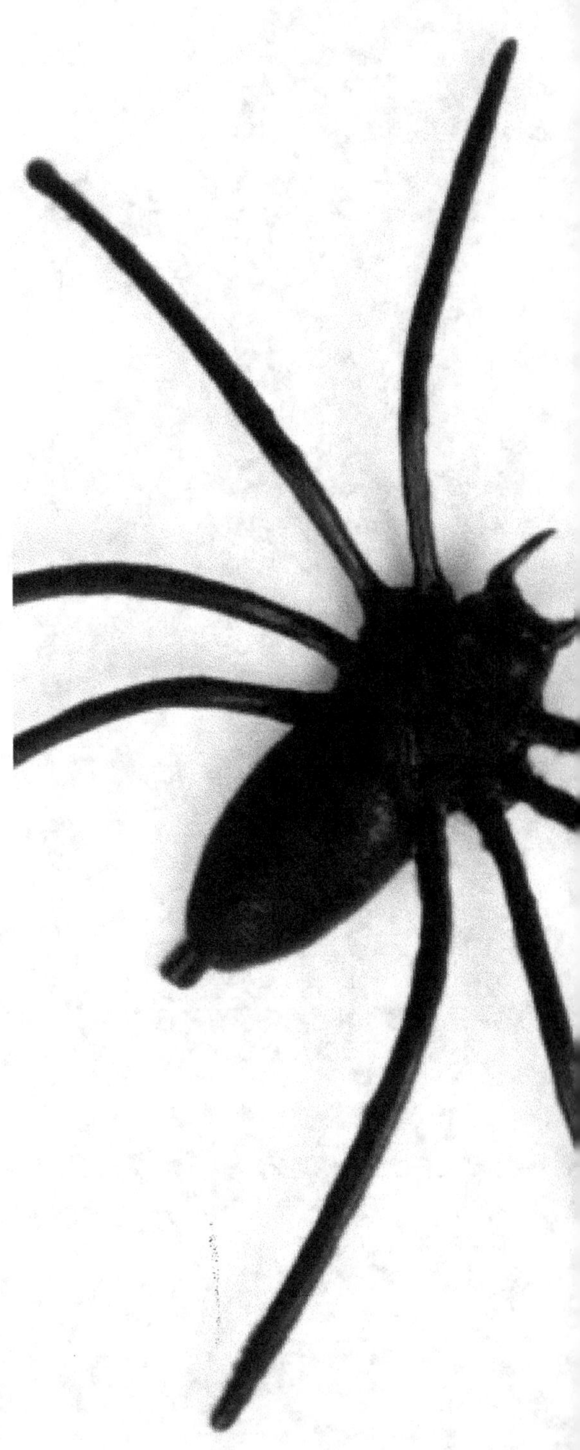

the design is delicate, use the spatula tool or your fingers to rub the letters down the sock before starting
to peel the design). You now have a cool pair of socks
that might look like the picture below!

HALLOWEEN T-SHIRT

MATERIALS NEEDED:

-T-shirt Blanks
-Glam Halloween SVG Files
-Cardstock
-Transfer Sheets (Black and Pink)
-Butcher Paper (comes with Infusible Ink rolls)
-LightGrip Mat
-EasyPress (12" x 10" size recommended)
-EasyPress Mat
-Lint Roller

DIRECTION

Import the SVG files into Cricut Design Space, and arrange them as you want them on the T-shirt.
Change the sizes of the designs to get them to fit on
the T-shirt.
Using the slice tool, slice the pink band away from
the hat's bowler part (the largest piece). Make a copy
of this band, and then slice it from the lower part of
the hat. With these done, you have three pieces that
fit together.
You can change the designs' colors as you would like
them. When you are done with the preparation, click
'Make It.'
Ensure that you invert your image using the 'Mirror'
toggle. This is even more important if there is text on

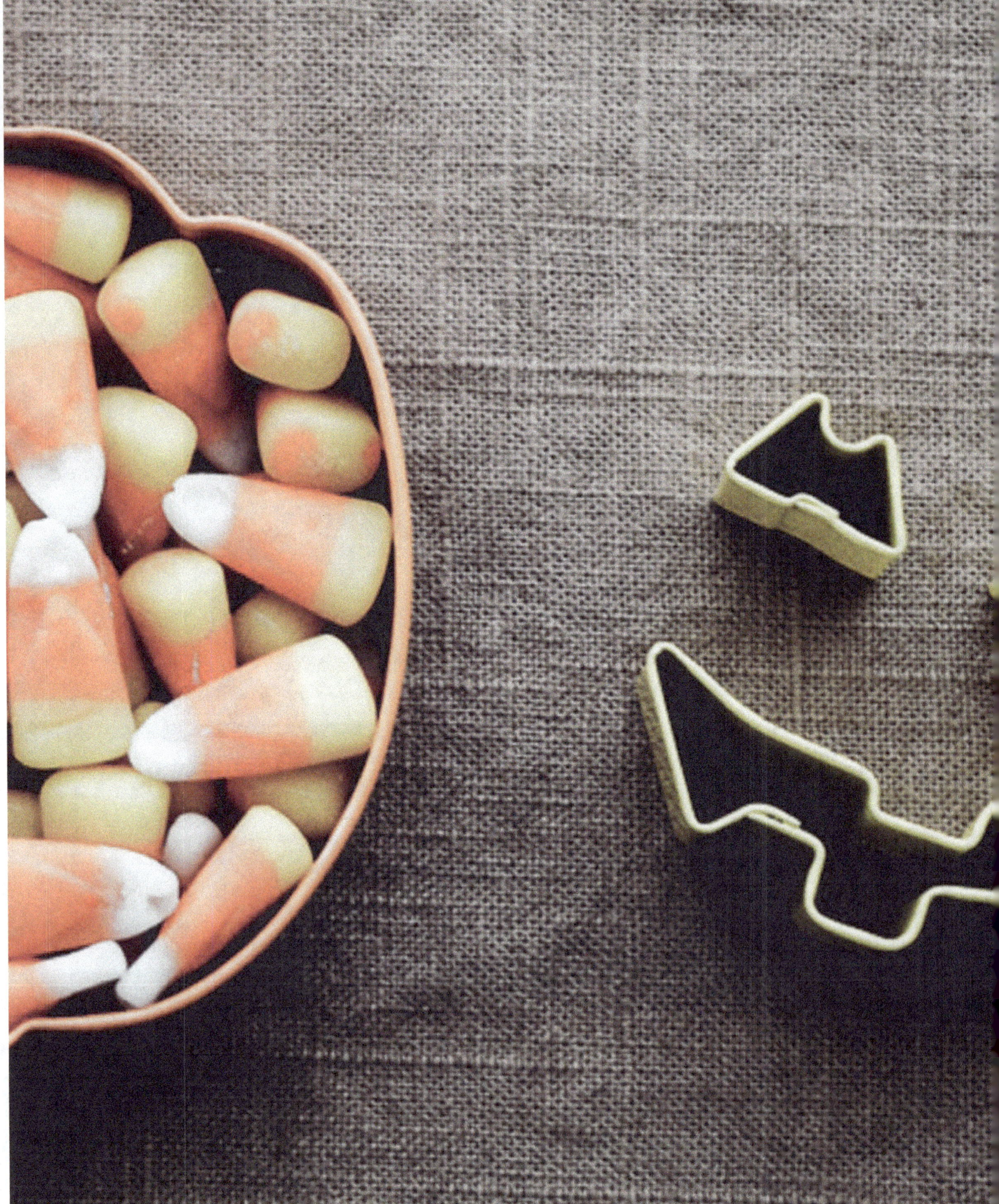

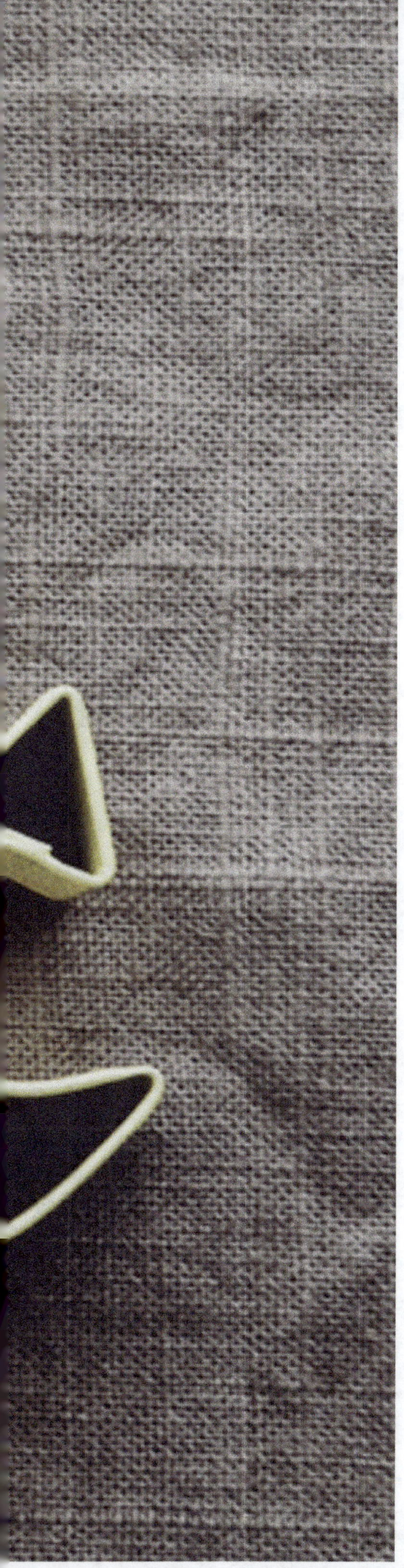

your design, as infusible ink designs should be done in inverse. This is because the part with the ink is to go right on the destination material.

Click on 'Continue.'

For the material, select 'Infusible Ink.' After this, cut the design out using your Cricut Machine.

With the designs cut out, weed the transfer sheet.

Cut around the designs such that the transfer tape does not cover any part of the infusible ink sheet. Ensure that this is done well, as any part of the infusible ink that is not in contact with the fabric will not be transferred.

Preheat your EasyPress to 385 degrees, and set your EasyPress mat.

Prepare your T-shirt by placing it on the EasyPress mat, then using a lint roller to remove any lint from the front.

Insert the Cardstock in the T-shirt, between the front and back, just where the design will be. This will protect the other side of the T-shirt from having the Infusible Ink on it.

If necessary, use the lint roller on the T-shirt again, after which you should heat your shirt with EasyPress. Do this at 385 degrees for 15 seconds.

Turn the part where the design faces on the T-shirt. Place the butcher paper on the design, ensuring that the backing does not overlap the design.

Place the EasyPress over the design, and hold it in place for 40 seconds. Do not move the EasyPress around so that your design does not end up looking smudged.

Remove the EasyPress from the shirt, and remove the transfer sheet.

To layer colors, ensure that your cutting around the transfer sheet is done as close as possible, then repeat the previous three steps for each color. This will prevent the transfer sheet from removing part of the color on the previously transferred design.

SHIRTS (VINYL, IRON ON)

MATERIALS NEEDED:

-Cricut Machine
-T-shirt
-Iron on or heat transfer vinyl
-Fine point blade and light grip mat
-Weeding tools
-EasyPress (regular household iron works fine too, with a little extra work)
-Small towel and Parchment paper

DIRECTION

In preparing for this project, Cricut recommends that you prewash the cloth without using any fabric softener before applying the iron-on or heat transfer vinyl on it. Ensure that your T-shirt is dry and ready before you proceed.

On Cricut Design Space, create your design, or import your SVG as described in the section on importing images.

If you are using an SVG file, select it and click on 'Insert Images.' When you do this, the image will appear in the Design Space canvas area.

Then, you need to resize the image to fit the T-shirt. To do this, select all the elements, set the height and width in the edit panel area, or simply drag the handle on the lower right corner of the selection.

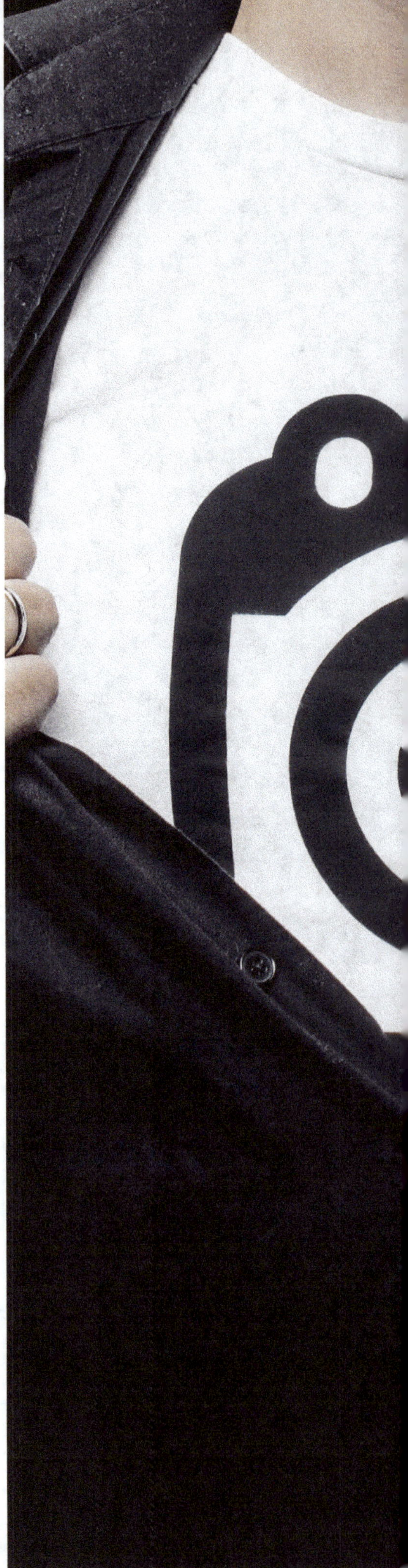

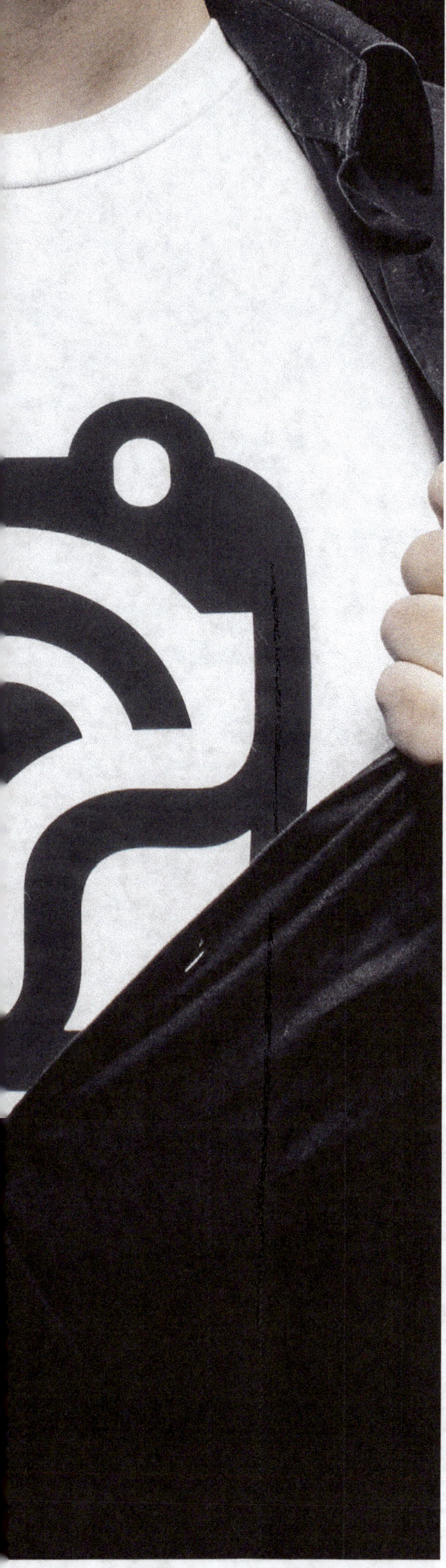

After this is done, select all the layers, click 'Attach' at the bottom of the 'Layers' panel, so the machine cuts everything as it is displayed on the canvas area. You can preview your design using Design Space's templates. You access this by clicking the icon called 'Templates' on the left panel of Design Space's canvas. There, you can choose what surface on which to visualize your design. Choose the color of your vinyl and the T-shirt so you can see how it will look once completed.

Once you are satisfied with the appearance of your design, click 'Make It.' If you have not connected your machine, you will be prompted to do so.

When the 'Prepare' page shows, there is a 'Mirror' option on the left panel. Ensure that you turn this on. This will make the machine cut it in reverse, as the top is the part that goes on to the T-shirt. Click 'Continue.'

Next, you are to select the material. When using the Cricut Maker, you will do this in Cricut Design Space. Choose 'Everyday Iron-On'. On Cricut Explore Air, you select the material using the smart set dial on the machine. Set this dial to 'Iron-On'.

Now, it is time to cut. To cut vinyl (and other such light materials), you should use the light-grip blue mat. Place the iron-on vinyl on the mat with the dull side facing up. Ensure that there are no bubbles on the vinyl; you can do this using the scraper.

Install the fine point blade in the Cricut machine, then load the mat with the vinyl on it by tapping the machine's small arrow. Then, press the 'Make It' button. When the machine is done cutting the vinyl, Cricut Design Space will notify you. When this happens, unload the mat.

With the cutting done, it is time to weed. This must

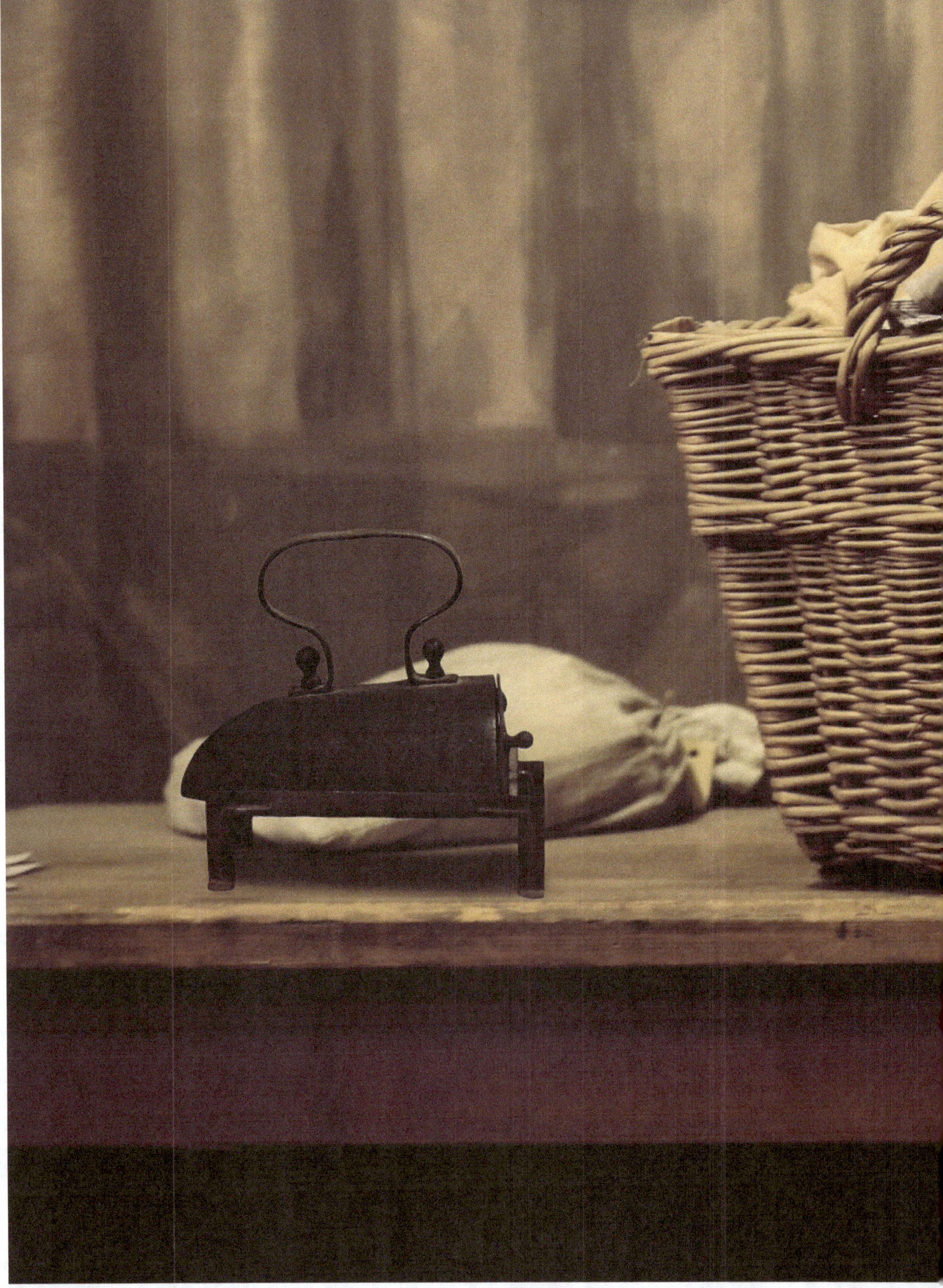

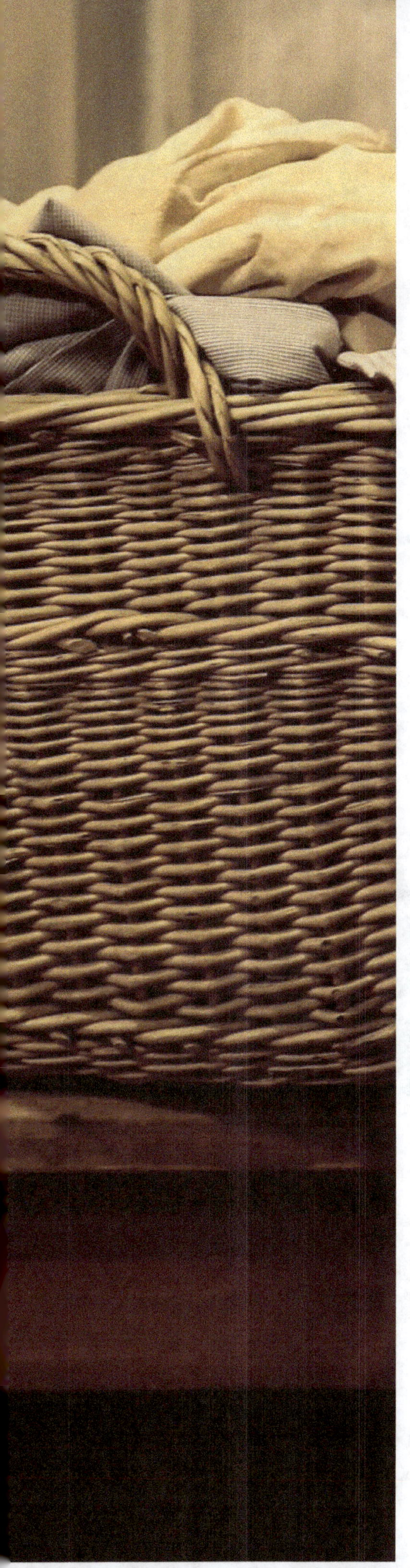

be done patiently so that you do not cut out the wrong parts. Therefore, you should have the design open as a guide.

After weeding, it is finally time to transfer the vinyl to the T-shirt. Before this, ensure that you have prewashed the T-shirt without fabric softener, as mentioned at the project's beginning.

To transfer the design, you can use EasyPress or a regular pressing iron. Using a pressing iron maybe a little more complicated, but it is certainly doable. Before you transfer, ensure that you have the EasyPress mat or a towel behind the material on to which you want to transfer the design to allow the material to be pressed harder against the heat.

Set the EasyPress to the temperature recommended on the Cricut heat guide for your chosen heat-transfer material and base material. For a combination of iron-on vinyl and cotton, the temperature should be set to 330°F. After preheating the EasyPress, get rid of wrinkles on the T-shirt and press the EasyPress on it for about 5 seconds. Then, place the design on the T-shirt and apply pressure for 30 seconds. After this, apply the EasyPress on the back of the T-shirt for about 15 seconds.

If you are using a pressing iron, the process is similar; only that you need to preheat the iron to max heat and place a thin cloth on the design, such that the iron does not have direct contact with the design or the T-shirt. This will prevent you from burning the T-shirt.

Wait for the design to cool off a bit, then peel it off while still a little warm.

Ensure that you wait for at least 24 hours after this before washing the T-shirt. When you do wash it, be sure to dry it inside out. Also, do not bleach the T-shirt.

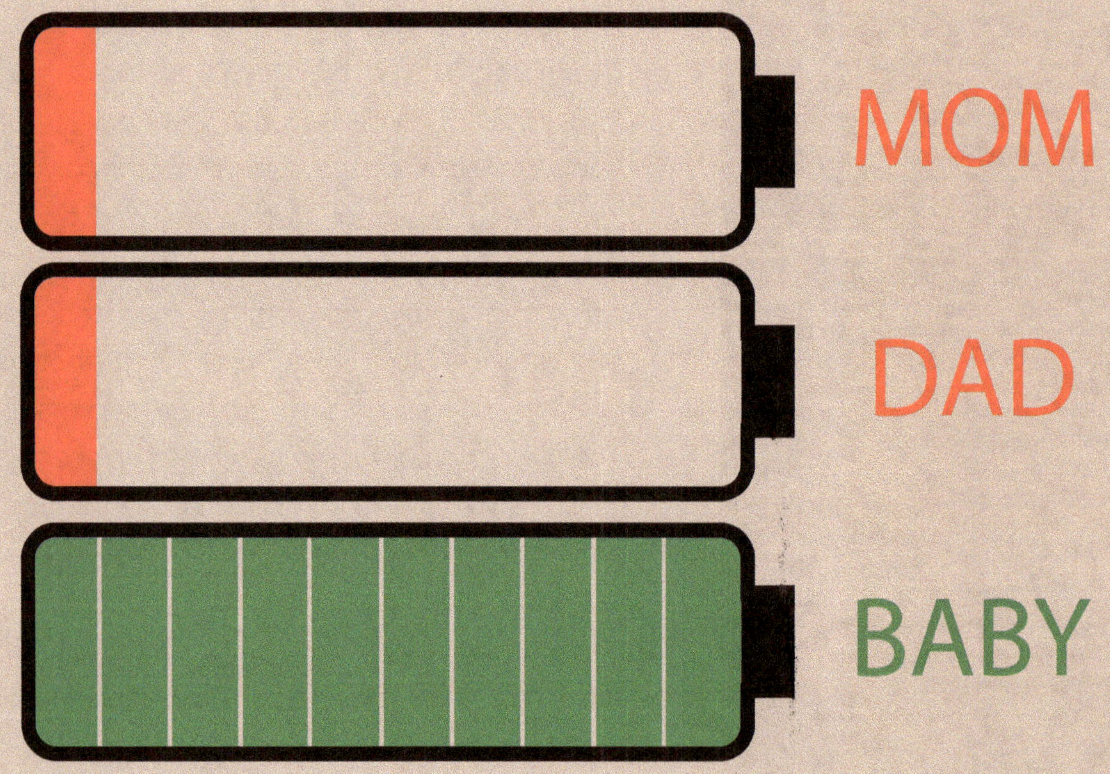

MOM
DAD
BABY

DAD JOKE VINYL T-SHIRT

MATERIAL NEEDED

-Your Favorite White Shirt
-Cricut Creator (or any other automated cutting machines using SVG files) or Discover Air 2 Cutting Machine
-Iron-On (Vinyl energy transfer) in different shades
-(Expressions of Cricut Vinyl)
-Instruments for weeding (Amazon Cricut)
-Easy Press 2 and Mat

DIRECTION

To keep making the "Dad Jokes?" I guess you're asking about RAD jokes! Hat, open Cricut Machine Space (or other device software) and append an SVG image.

Drop the imported picture onto a new canvas, size it to fit the shirt (we recommend making it around 10 "long for the shirt of a mature male), and in the upper right corner, click the green" Print it Now "icon."

The remaining vinyl is scraped off using the weeding equipment to remove the iron-on vinyl with the grinding machine.

Next, in the Online Quick reference source, use Easy Press 2 to apply the template to the top, observing the time and temperature configuration needed. Short, quick, and completely enjoyable! That will give

Dad a great present for Father's Day, Christmas, Birthdays, and more!

This approach even performed on a hat very well! Use your Sport Flex Iron-On adhesive or Infusible Ink and Easy Press Miniature on this polyester trucking cover for a super fun gift idea.

QUIVER AND ARROW

MATERIALS NEEDED

-{Use 4/20} "Wooden Round Dowels
{In the colors you would like the Cupid Arrows to be} Spray Paint
-Twine, Lace, Jute, or braided rope {whatever dowels you like to wrap with}
-Cylinder Jar ~ {I bought mine from Walmart} for your quiver.
-To adorn the bottle, Packaging Sheet or Print
-Paper
-Scrapbook Paper {I used gloss cardstock} in the colors you want the arrows and wings to be. You should use a matching scrap of paper.

DIRECTIONS

Brush the dowels with color.
To achieve the perfect look, hot glue the ribbon on the dowel {I twisted mine and hot fused both ends}.
Cut out the arrow and feather
Apply hot glue to the arrows and feathers

DIRECTIONS FOR QUIVER

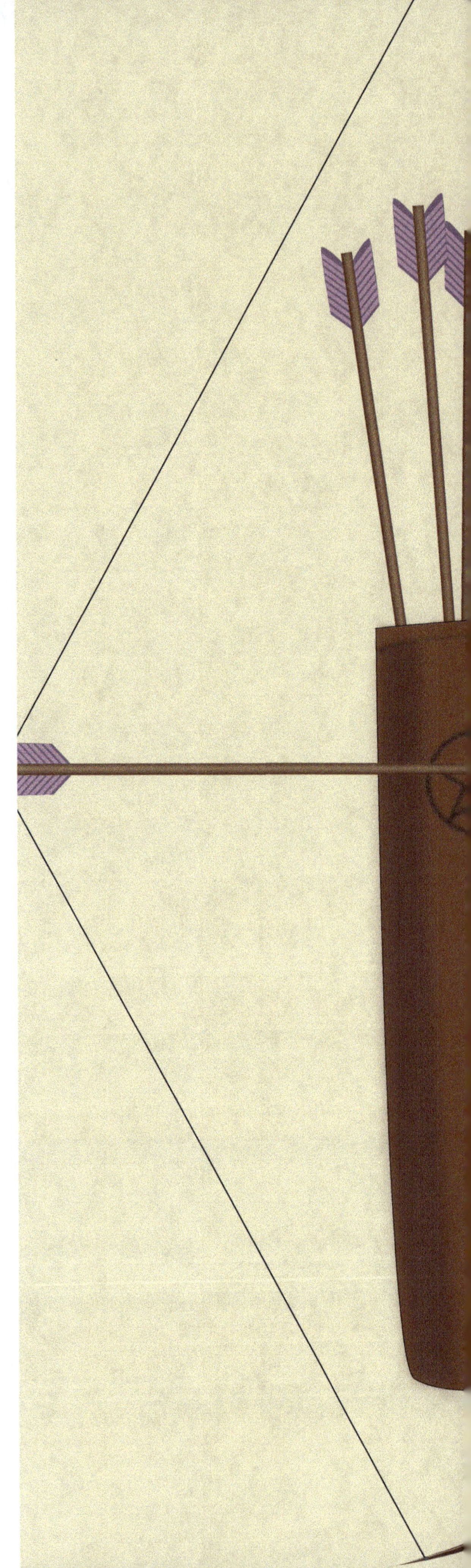

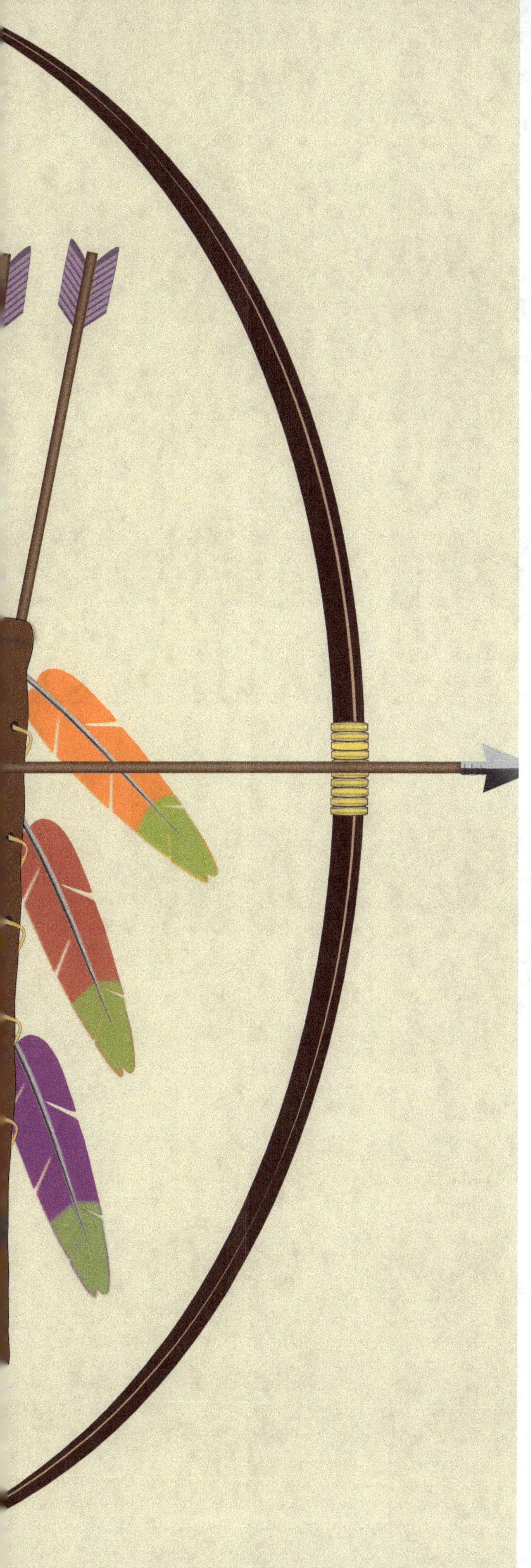

Cut the paper to the width and length of the cylinder {scrapbook or wrapping}
Fasten the document to the cylinder
To hold the Cupid Arrows in place, insert the corresponding paper shred inside to
If you'd like to add a matching brace.
Now you can put the Cupid Wings anywhere you can, it will look amazing on a door or wall, and your buddies will ask you to make them more! These are beloved by both my kiddos and they both have a collection in their bed.

ST. PATRICK'S DAY SHIRT

MATERIALS NEEDED

-Machine to cut Cricut maker
-Cricut Space Development account
-Cut design with shamrock and doodles
Infusible Pen Ink 0.04-Green
-Cricut Space Access Design
-Infusible Cricut Tin Jacket
-Easy Press 2 Print
-Card Warehouse
-Butcher Text
-Paper on Laser Printer
-They have arranged the Cricut Room canvas to help you get started with this St. Patrick's Day Top!

DIRECTIONS

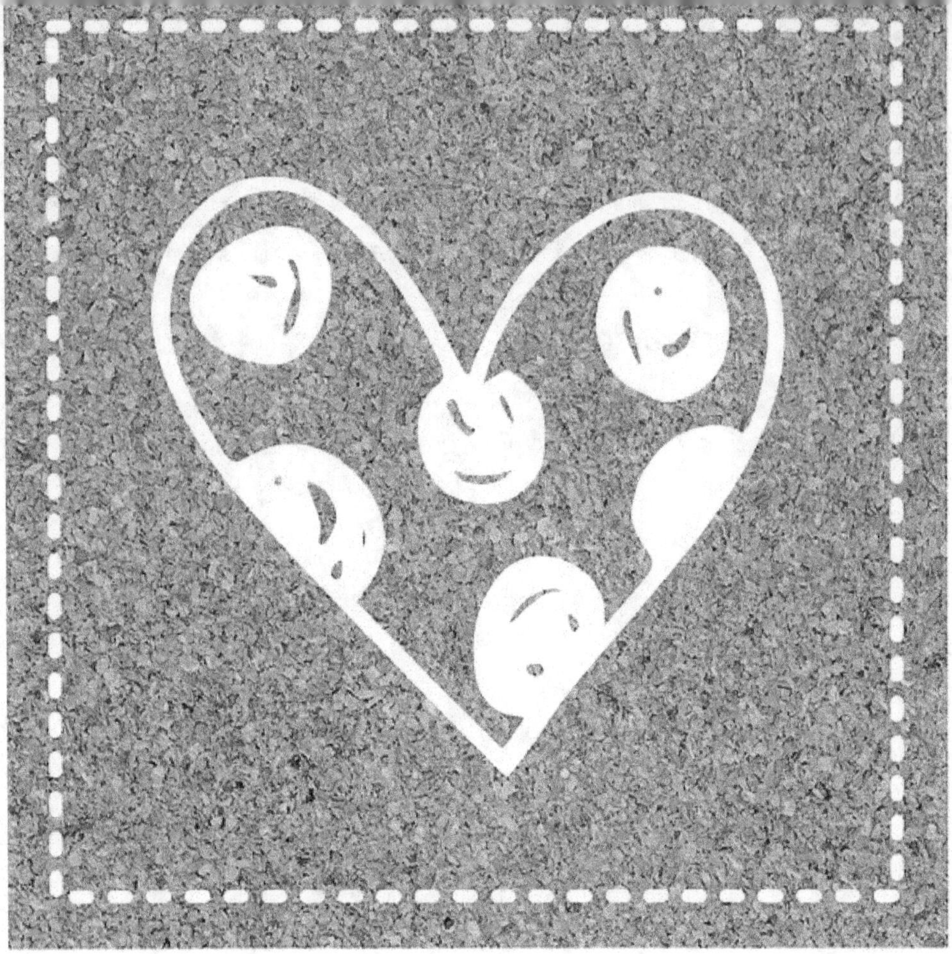

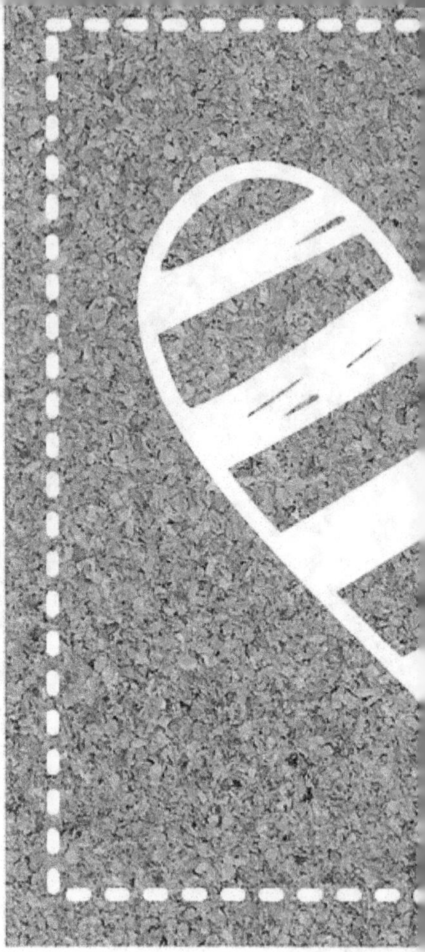

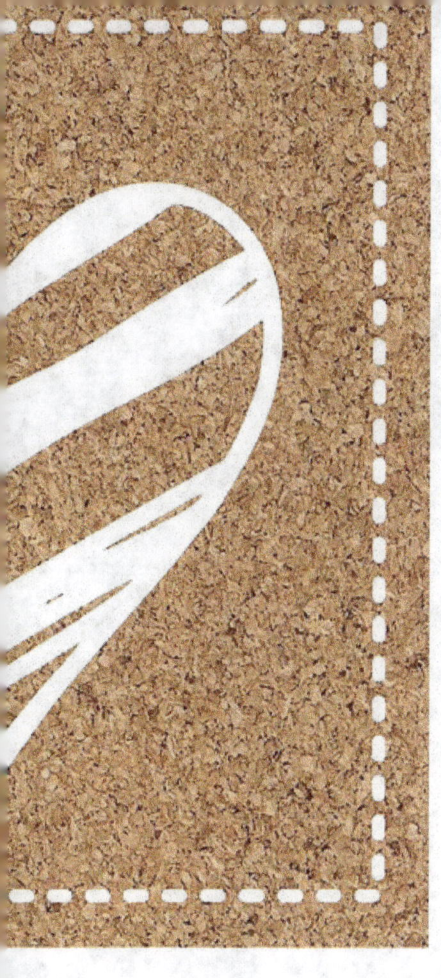

Activate and size the Design Space Cut File to fit your shirt.

Send out to cut (draw) the project. Don't forget to have an image mirror. Place the paper with Laser Printer on a standard grip cutting mat. Keep sure to follow the Infusible Ink Pen prompts.

Delete the laser printer paper from the cutting mat once the image has been drawn.

Place a cardstock sheet inside the shirt where you want your design to be.

Place on the shirt, image side down, the laser printer paper with design.

Cover butcher paper to the laser printer.

Following Cricut's recommended heat setting, press the image onto the shirt with the Easy Press.

Remove from the shirt the butcher paper, laser printer paper, and card stock and be St. Paddy's Day pinch-proof

If we're acquainted with the cutting Cricut device family, you're likely familiar with all of the various projects done by you with these instruments, too. The electronic cutting machine or Cricut Joy appears to fit in the right with many types of material that the cutting tool can cut.

COASTERS USING INFUSIBLE INK FOR CHRISTMAS

MATERIALS NEEDED

-Maker Cricut or Explore
-Infusible Ink rounds from Ceramic Coasters
-Buffalo Plaid (Infusible Ink Transmission Sheets)
-Easy Press
-Mat from Easy Press
-Butcher's Article

-Cardstock White

DIRECTIONS:

The prototypes accessible in Design Space with the terms 'Everything is good' and "All is Light" were photos
On the tile coasters, the Infusible Ink appears so shiny and glossy. I think they'd be great in your house as holiday decor or attach them to a gift package of mugs and hot chocolate.
Open the Space File for Christmas Coaster Concept. Print out the patterns from the move sheets of Infusible Paint. Don't hesitate to get the concept replicated.
Weed the layouts.
Click, in the Heat Guide, to obey the instructions. With a sheet of cardstock underneath the coasters and a parchment paper strip over the Infusible Paint's edge, push for 220 seconds at 390 degrees. Once the coaster has settled, gently cut the transfer cover.

CLEAR PERSONALIZED LABELS

MATERIALS NEEDED

-Cricut clear sticker paper
-High-gloss printer paper for the Inkjet printer
-Inkjet printer (check the ink cartridges
-Spatula tool

DIRECTION

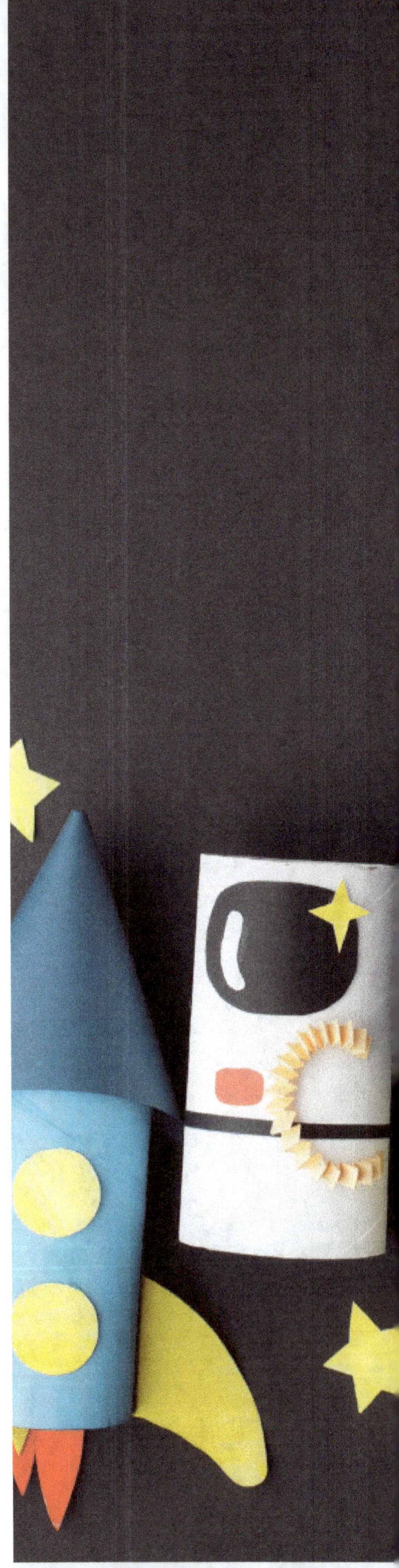

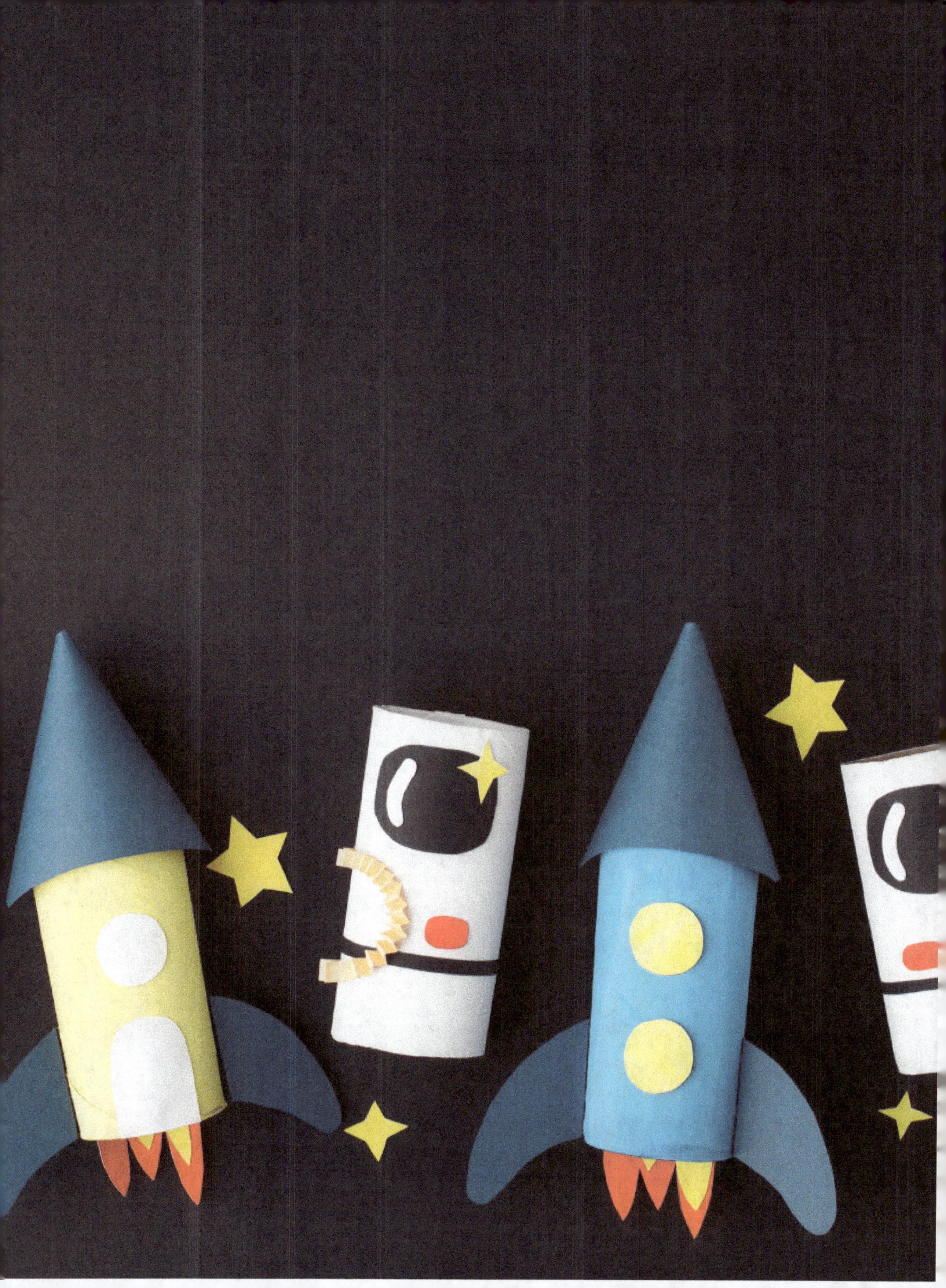

Create a new project in Design Space.

Choose the heart shape from the left-hand side Shapes menu.

Select an image from the Images menu on the left-hand side menu.

Choose a picture of a flower or search for 'M55E.' Unlock the flower image, position it in the top-left corner of the heart. Make sure it fits without any overhang.

Select the heart and the flower, then click on Weld from the bottom-right-hand menu. This ensures that the label is printed together as a unit and not in layers.

Select the heart and flowers once again. Then click on Flatten to ensure that only the outline shape of the heart is cut out.

Choose Text from the left-hand menu. Choose a font, and type the text for your label. You can choose a color for your text.

Unlock and move the text into position in the middle of the label.

Adjust the size to fit comfortably.

Select the heart shape and the font. Then click on Flatten to ensure the label is cut as a whole and not layered.

To not waste sticker paper, you will want to print as many labels per sheet as you can.

Choose the square shape from the Shapes menu. Position it on the screen, unlock the shape, and set the measurements to a width of 6″ and a height of 9″.

Move the first label into place at the top-left-hand corner of the screen.

Select the label and Duplicate it.

Move the second label next to the first one. Give

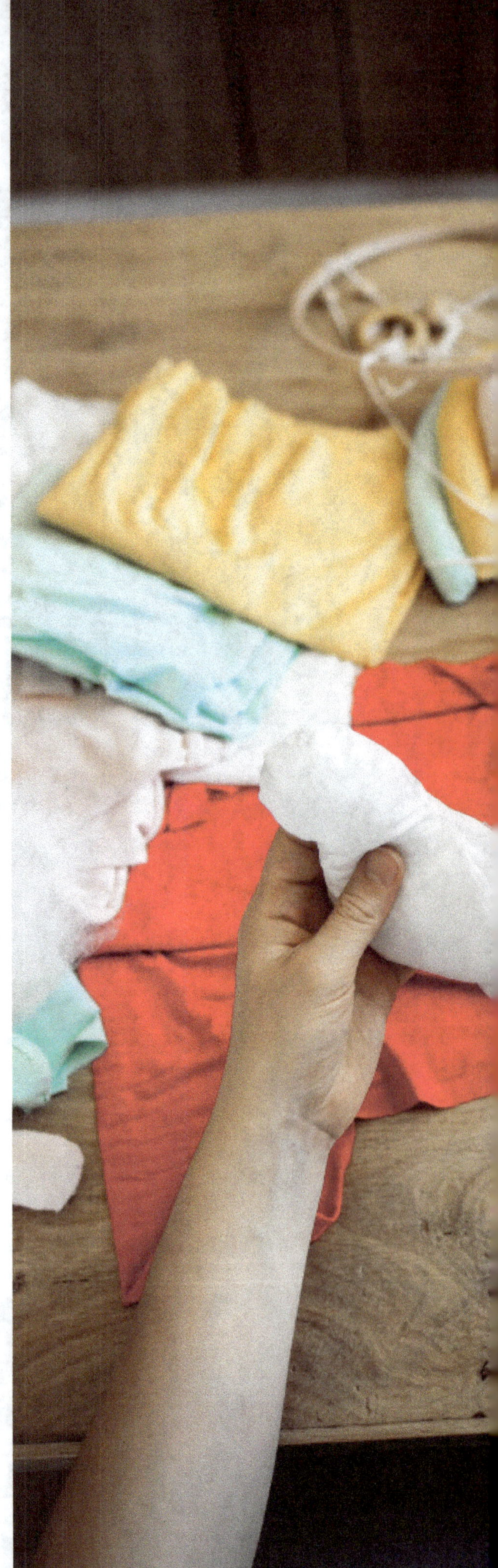

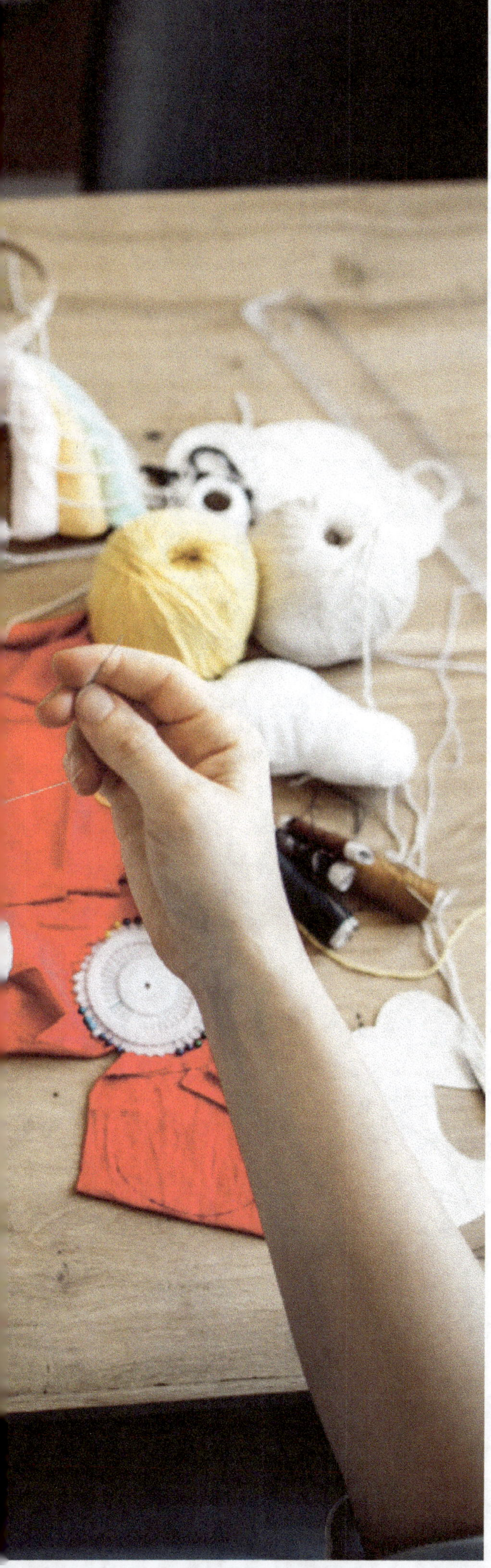

the labels a bit of room between each other and the edges.

Fit as many as you can on the sheet, then save your work.

Fill in each of the labels with the text you want. If you have space left over when your labels are positioned, you can create smaller ones.

You can create all different sizes of labels, patterns, and designs.

Make sure that all the labels are for print and are flattened.

Delete the background rectangle.

Select all the labels, and click Attach from the bottom-right-hand menu.

Click Make it, and check that the design and wording are correct before clicking Continue.

Choose the high-gloss paper option, and set it to the best quality.

Load the sticker paper into the Inkjet printer, and press Send to printer.

Choose Sticker paper for the Cricut materials.

Load the Stickers into the Cricut, and press Go when it is ready to cut.

The Cricut will cut out the stickers, so you can peel them off the backing sheet as and when you need them.

CUSTOM COASTERS

MATERIALS NEEDED:

-Free Pattern Templates
-Monogram Design (in Design Space)
-Cardstock, or Printing Paper
-Butcher Paper

-Lint-free towel
-Round Coaster Blanks
-Light Grip Mat
-EasyPress 2 (6" x 7" recommended)
-EasyPress Mat
-Infusible Ink Pens
-Heat Resistant Tape
-Cricut BrightPad (optional), for easier tracking

DIRECTION

In Cricut Design Space, open the monogram design. You can click 'Customize', choose the designs that you want to cut out, or just go ahead and cut out all the letters.
Click on 'Make It'.
On the page displayed, click on 'Mirror Image' to make the image mirrored. This must be done whenever you are using infusible ink. For your material, choose 'Cardstock'. Then, place your cardstock on the mat, load it into the machine, then press the 'Cut' button on the Cricut machine.
After the Cricut machine is done cutting, unload it and remove the done monograms from the mat.
Trace the designs onto the cut-out. If you have a Cricut Bright Pad, you can use it to carry out this step much more efficiently, as it will make the trace lines easier to identify. Tracing should be done using Cricut Infusible Ink Pens.
Use the lint-free towel to wipe the coaster. Ensure that no residue is left behind to prevent any marks from being left on the blank.
Make the design centered on the face down

coaster.

Get a piece of butcher paper about an inch larger on each side of the coaster and place it on top of the design.

Tape this butcher paper onto the coaster using heat-resistant tape to hold the design fast.

Set the temperature of your EasyPress to 400 degrees and set the timer to 240 seconds.

Place another butcher paper piece on your EasyPress mat, set the coaster on top of it, face up.

Place another piece of butcher paper on top of these. Place the already preheated EasyPress on top of the coaster and start the timer.

Lightly hold the EasyPress in place (without moving) or leave it in place right on the coaster - if on a perfectly flat surface - till the timer goes off.

After this is done, gently remove the EasyPress 2, then turn it off.

The coaster will be very hot, so you should leave it to get calm before touching it. When it is cool, you can peel the design off of it.

Chapter 6
Basswood chipboard balsa wood

WOODEN HAND-LETTERED SIGN

MATERIALS NEEDED

Acrylic paint, in whatever colors you would like
Vinyl Cricut Explore Air 2
Walnut, hollow basswood planks
Transfer Tape
Scraper
An SVG file or font that you wish to use
Pencil
Eraser

DIRECTION

You will need to start by deciding what you will want to draw onto the wood.

Then, place some lines on the plank to designate the horizontal and vertical axis for the grid. Set this aside for later.

Upload the file that you wish to use to the Design Space. Then, cut the file with the proper setting for vinyl.

Weed out the writing or design spaces that are

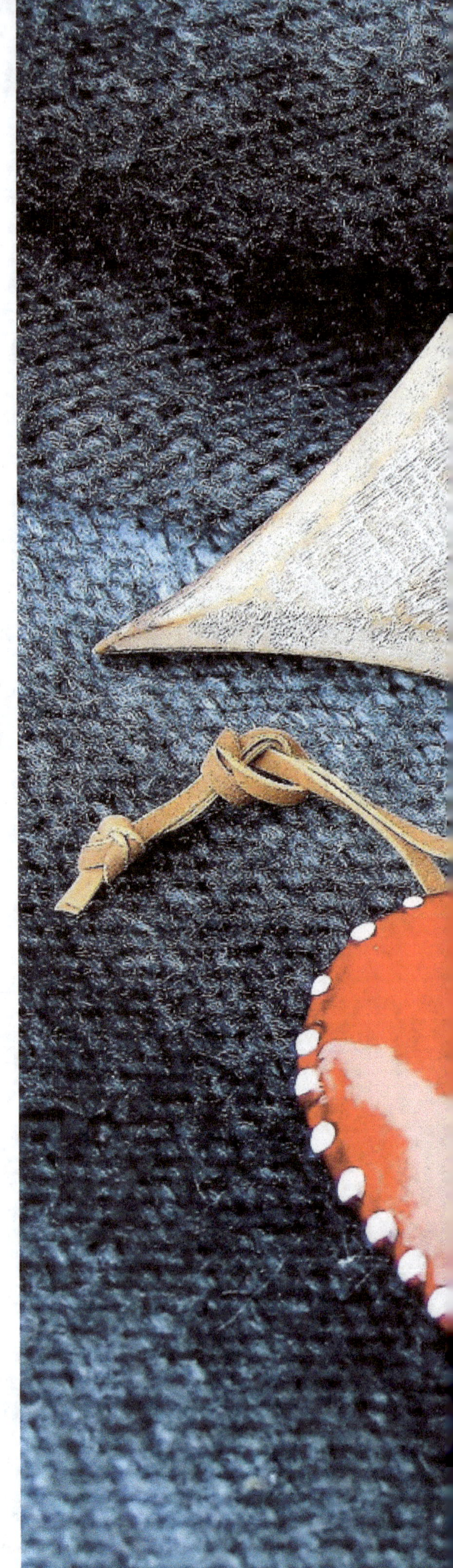

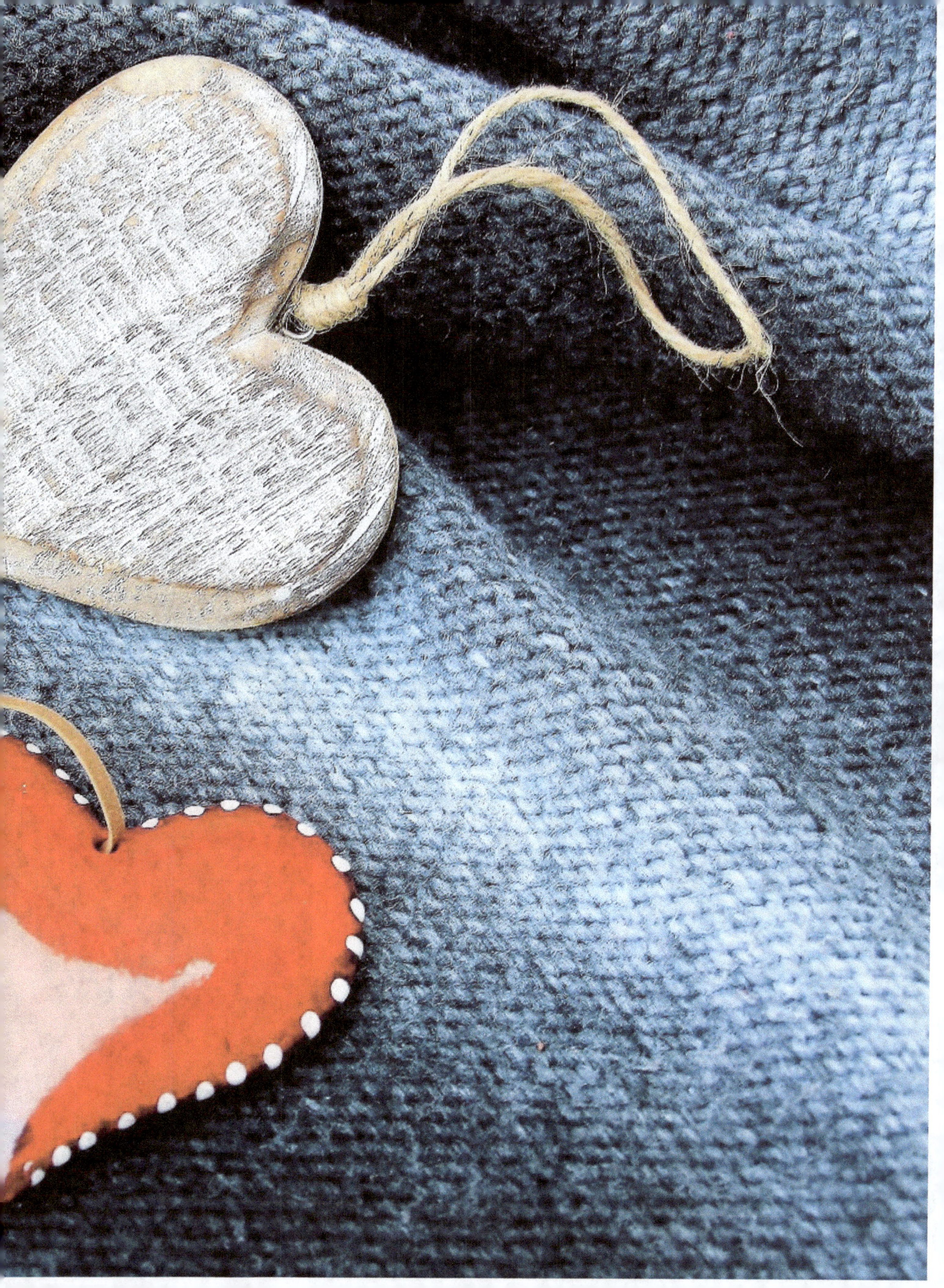

not meant to go on the wood.

Using the transfer tape, apply the tape to the top of the vinyl, and smooth it. Using the scraper and the transfer paper's corner, slowly peel the backing off a bit at a time. Do it carefully.

Remove the vinyl pieces' backing, aligning the lettering or design so that it is entirely centered. Place it carefully on the wooden plank.

Again, use the scraper to smooth out the vinyl on the plank.

Take off the transfer tape by smoothing off the bubbles as you scrape along with the wood sign. Discard the transfer tape at that time.

Continue to use the scraper to make the vinyl smoother. There should be no bumps since this creates bleeding.

Now, paint your wood plank with any color of your choice. Peel the vinyl letters off. Once the paint has completely dried, you can erase your pencil marks.

WOODEN GIFT TAGS

MATERIALS NEEDED

Balsa wood
Gold vinyl
Vinyl transfer tape
Cutting mat
Weeding tool or pick

DIRECTION

Secure your small balsa wood pieces to the cutting mat, then tape the edges with masking tape for

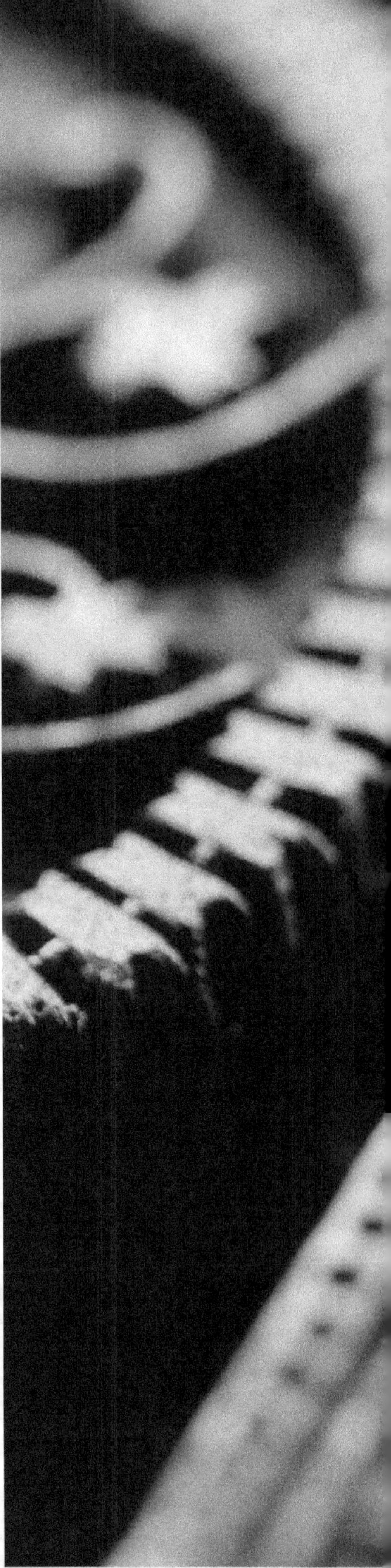

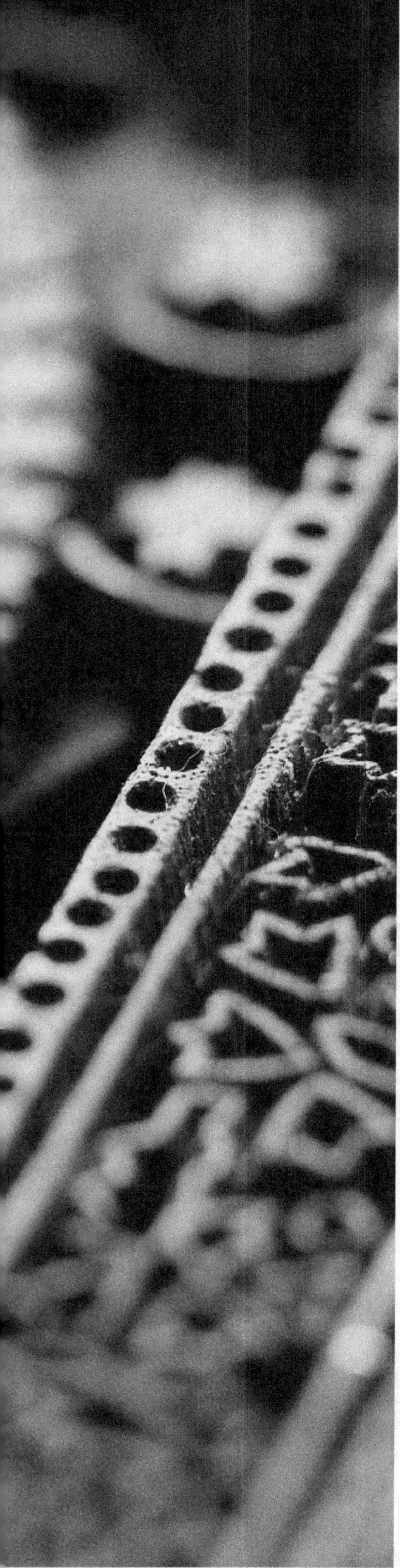

additional strength.

Open Cricut Design Space and create a 'New Project'.

Select the shape you would like for your tags, set the Cricut to cut wood, then send the design to the Cricut.

Remove your wood tags from the Cricut, and remove any excess wood.

In Cricut Design Space, select the 'Text' button in the lower left-hand corner.

Choose your favorite font, and type the names you want to place on your gift tags.

Place your vinyl on the cutting mat.

Send the design to your Cricut.

Use a weeding tool, or pick to remove the excess vinyl from the text.

Apply transfer tape to the quote.

Remove the paper backing from the tape.

Place the names on the wood tags.

Rub the tape to transfer the vinyl to the wood, making sure there are no bubbles. Carefully peel the tape away.

Thread twine or string through the holes and decorate your gifts

CHARMING DRIFTWOOD SIGN

MATERIALS NEEDED

Wood plank
Some Paint
Vinyl
Piece of rope

DIRECTION

Select an appropriate size of a wooden piece with some suitable length as you are using it, so it's totally up to you which size you prefer.

Draw a shape and image on a piece of paper. Place this image on the wooden plank and draw the shape using a paper image as a stencil with some prominent marker color.

Paint the image or letter with any bright color or with any color of your choice.

In the final step, add vinyl covering. It is ready to use, now pass some thread, rope, or any other hanging material.

PARTY DECOR MEDALLIONS

MATERIALS NEEDED

Records- 45 same size
Posterboard
Scale
Scissors
Adhesive/Glue
Vintage Milk Caps
Twine
Scrapbook
Scallop Punch

DIRECTION

In the first step, measurements are made, and cutting is applied to paper. Fold many papers and cut them in once, paper with measurement of

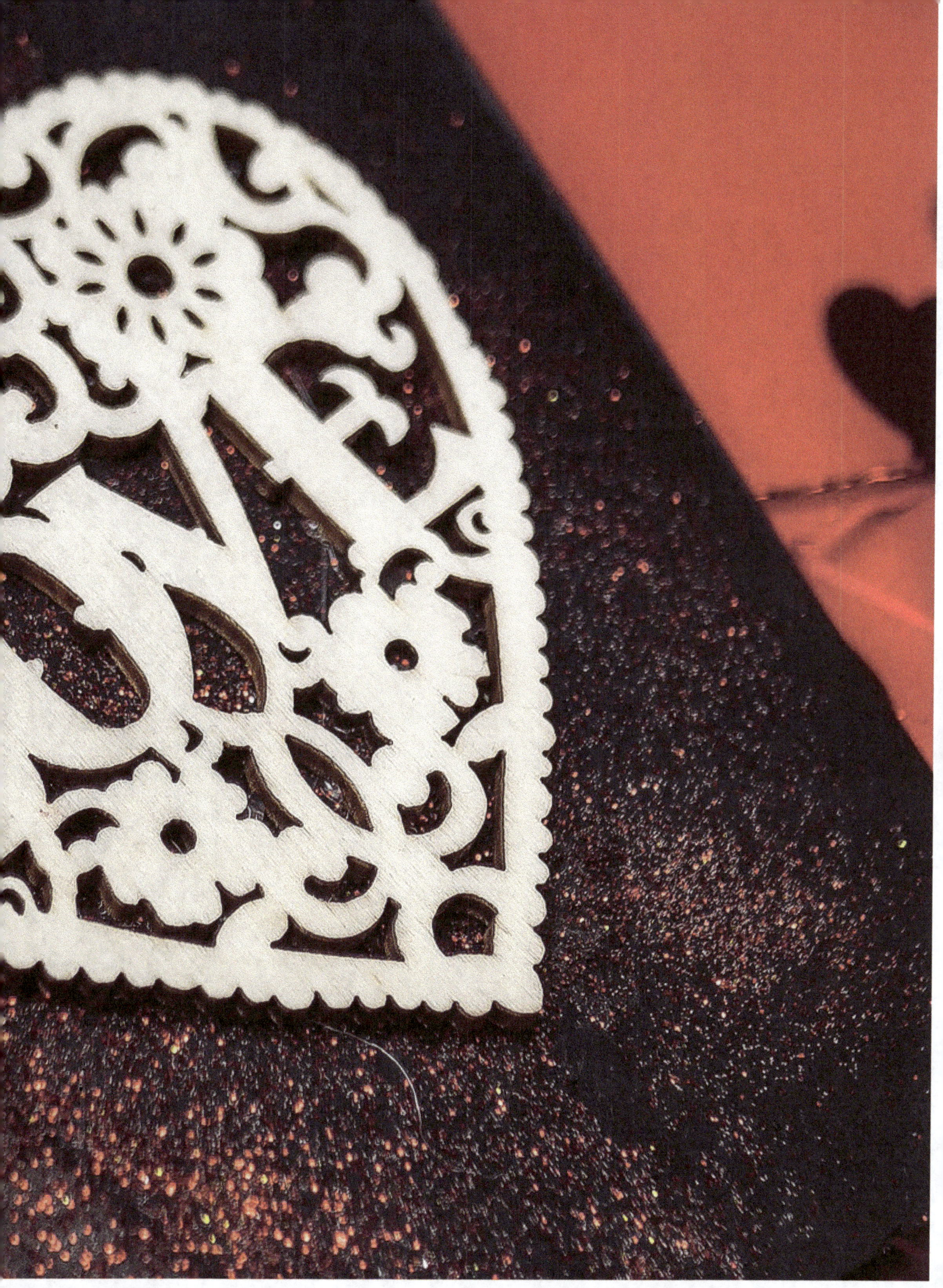

6,5,4 inches in width for small, medium, and large medallions.

By holding one end of the paper, fold it, repeat the folds backward and fourth ward. All of the paper strips should be folded in the same way.

Now attach all of the strips with the help of glue but how they become in the form of seamless strip.

Squeeze the strips from the end and pull all of the strips to form them in a shape of a circle. By using glue, take the record and attach it from the lower portion of the paper medallion. Now take 2.5 scallops and fix them with each other.

Apply some glue to the center and fix the milk cap and center of the circle. On the backside of the center top of the medallion, attach a twine piece; pass a string into it; now it is ready for hanging on the wall or in any other place.

CHALKBOARD CALENDAR

MATERIAL NEEDED

Wooden board
Wooden filler
Scale
Paints
Cutter

DIRECTION

A large cardboard piece, any used cardboard can be reused. Use some wood filler to fill or fix the holes, if any. Paint the board with any of your fa-

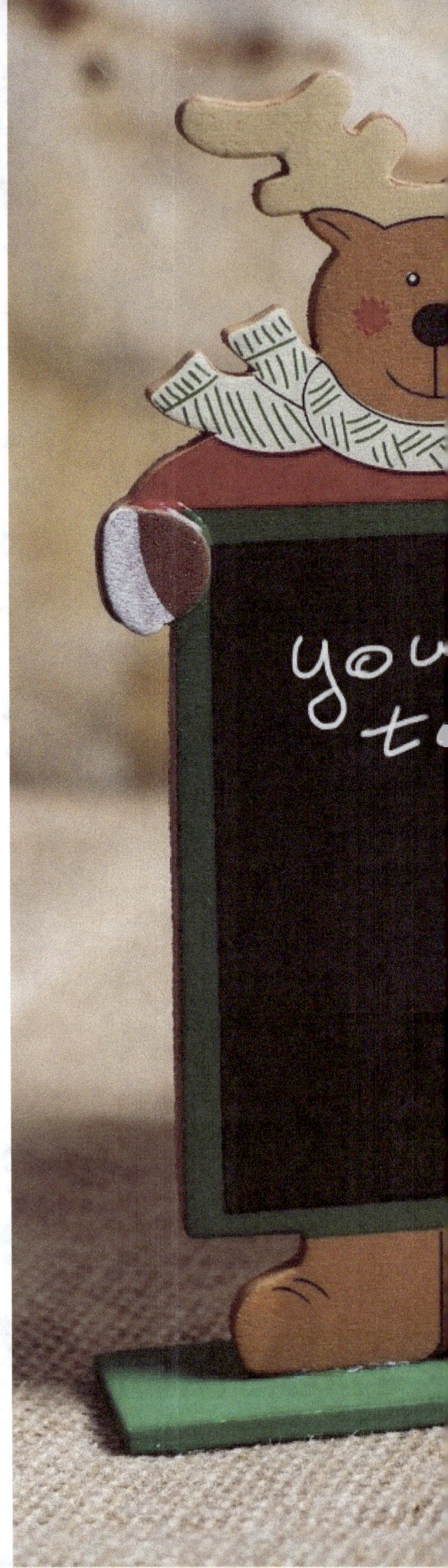

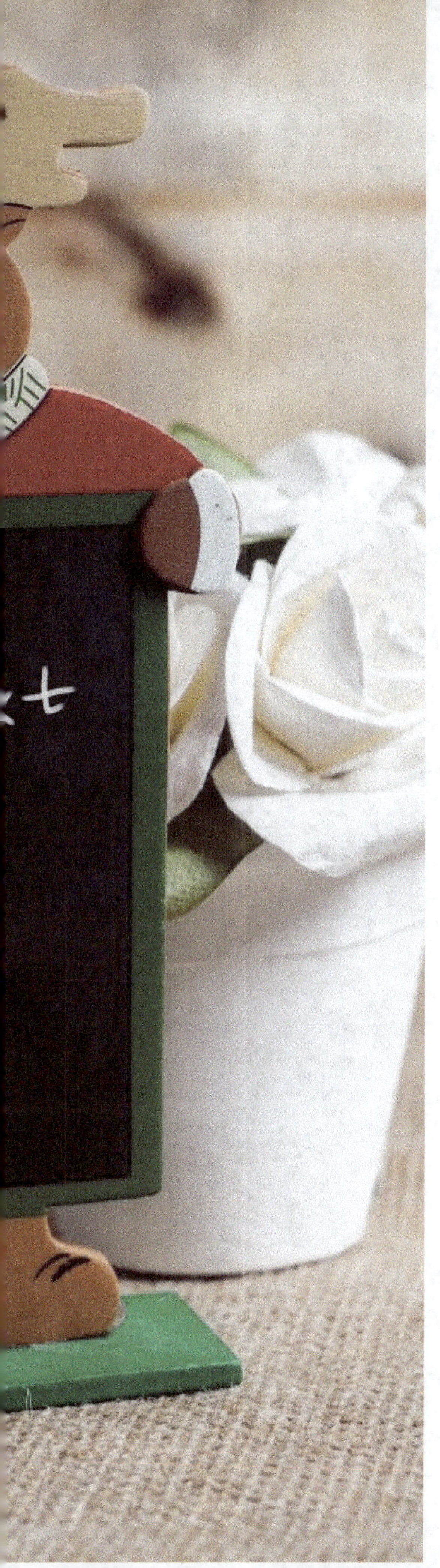

vorite or desired colors.
By using Silhouette, SD cut the chalkboard and carefully draw some squares with exact measurements. Mark the area by using chalk ink markers.
Now make some holders by using the Mason jar and pipe clamp. You can assign any sign or add any of tags and any kind of references to it.

FAMILY BIRTHDAY WOODEN BOARD

MATERIAL NEEDED

Wooden Board
Chalk Paints
Paint Brushes
Finishing Cloths
Plastic Gloves
Sandpapers
Old Rags
Lettering vinyl

DIRECTION

Apply a coat of chalk paint to the wooden board, let it dry.
Then do another coating of paint for a refined look. Give some time, like two hours, to complete its drying period. Now take some wood finishing cloth. By using an old rug, wipe all of the extra paint. Then give again some time to get it dry. Designing family members' names and counting age numbers style of quoting them is a personal choice. Very slightly and carefully use sandpaper.
Now apply the vinyl in lettering. The color and desi-

gn of the letter are totally up to your choice.

Pallet sign

Material needed

Scrapbook paper in the colors of your choice

Mod podge

Paper trimmer

Paintbrush.

Using your Mod Podge, coat the wood boards and the backside of your triangles.

Place the triangles one at a time on the board, coating the top with another thin coat of Mod Podge. Allow your sign to completely dry, and then give it a final coat of Mod Podge.

That is it. The last tip, if you are looking for pallet sign ideas, 48✕40 has tons of them on the internet.

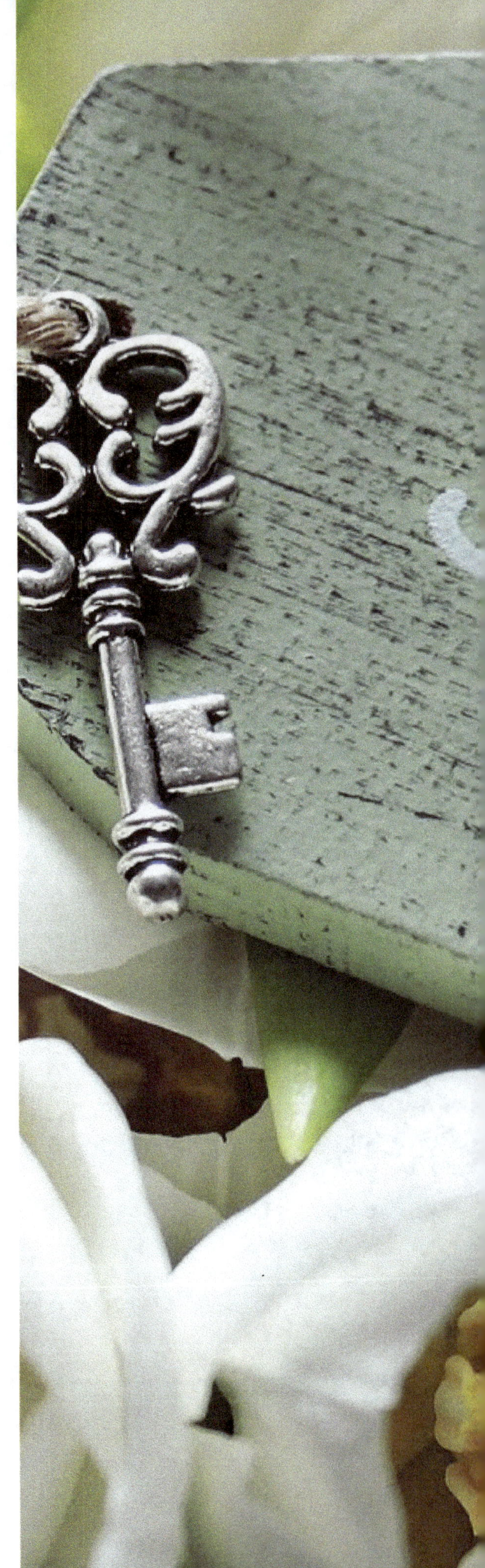

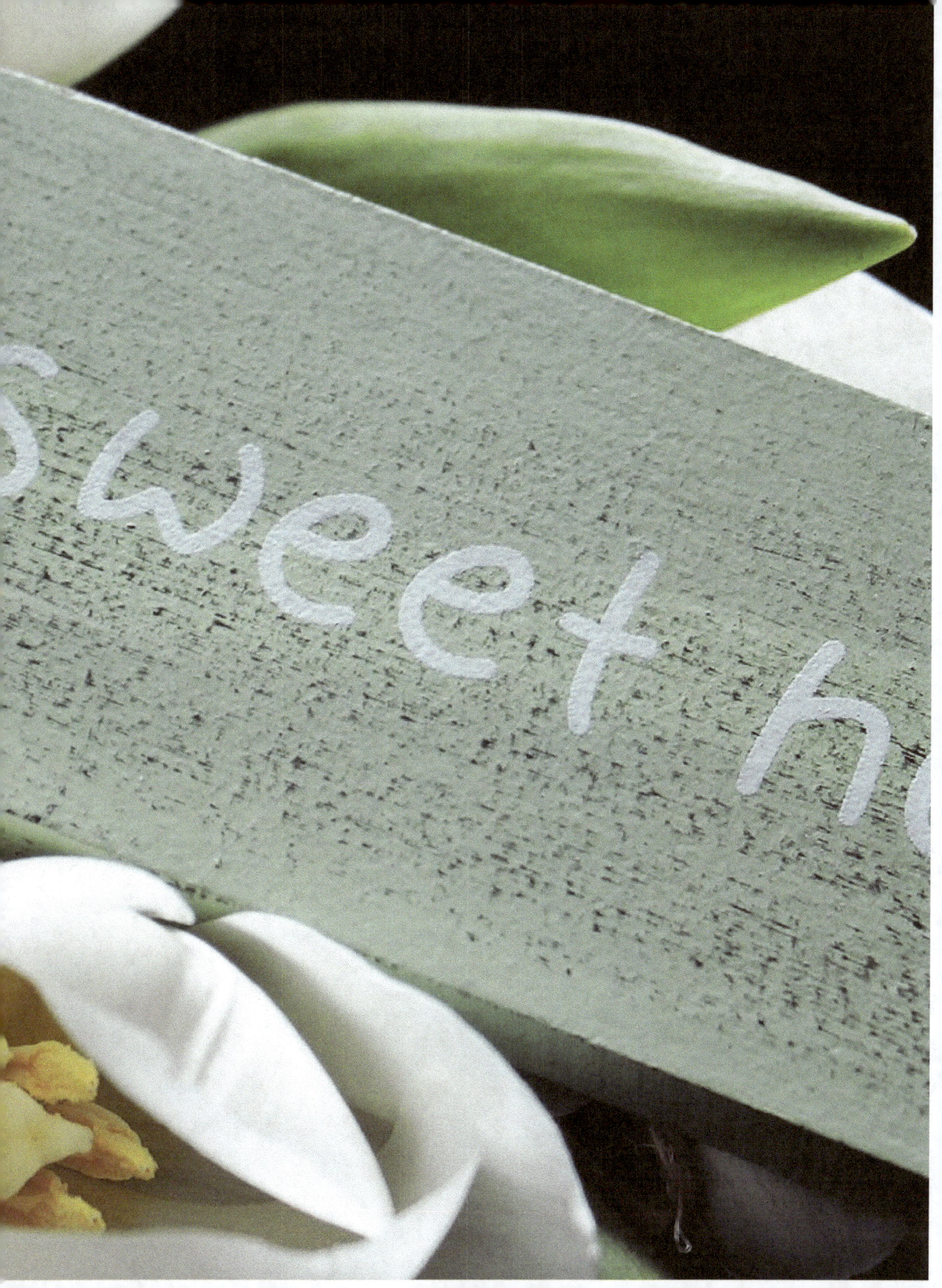
sweet h

Conclusion

Here is Sienna Tally writing to you!

Given the breadth of projects I'd like to offer you the adventure doesn't end here! In fact, I'll be back soon with another guide dedicated to materials and individual occasions. It's time to get crafting! Enjoy your new knowledge of your fantastic machine and give a new project a try. The beauty of the Cricut is the versatility of functions and user-friendly format. Use this to make your life and home and those of your friends and family more exciting and beautiful!

Now that you have completed this handy manual on using the Cricut machine, you should be well-equipped to head out into the Cricut crafting world and start designing your favorite crafts today. With each single Cricut cartridge, you can set up a specific image or design that you can reuse every day. There are a few limitations, but mostly it is how high your imagination can go.

So, make that card, cut those felt flowers, a design that excellent quotable sign, or create some lovely new earrings for you or your best friend to wear. Whatever it is that you want to create, the Cricut has gotten you covered with the machine's versatility. If you need a portable one, you are in luck since the Cricut Mini is designed to go with you anywhere you have internet and a computer.

As you gain more experience using the computer and try new features, you can solve almost all of them.

The next step is to find projects and materials that excite you and dive right in! It would be great to see you embrace the vast number of crafting opportunities that now lie ahead of you.

Tweak the ideas in this book to fit you perfectly. Change up the materials, the blanks, what the design is, and whatever else your imagination can come up with. Create your projects, as well. Following the ideas in this book will give you a good foundation for using your Cricut. Once you've become familiar with it in the different ways you can use it, you can let your creativity flow and create whatever you want.

HAPPY CRAFTING

Thank you !!

www.ingramcontent.com/pod-product-compliance
Lightning Source LLC
Chambersburg PA
CBHW080456030726
47592CB00011B/3145